Benjamin Haas an

111 Places in Buenos Aires That You Must Not Miss

111

emons:

Para Nora y Alfredo

Para nuestros queridos amigos y amigas de Argentina

Special thanks to everyone who supported us,
without whom this book would be only half as exciting.

Layout: Eva Kraskes, based on a design
by Lübbeke | Naumann | Thoben
Maps: altancicek.design, www.altancicek.de
Basic cartographical information from Openstreetmap,
© OpenStreetMap-Mitwirkende, ODbL
English translation: John Sykes
Printing and binding: Lensing Druck GmbH & Co. KG,
Feldbachacker 16, 44149 Dortmund
Printed in Germany 2018
ISBN 978-3-7408-0260-8
First edition

Foreword

Many documentaries and reports on Buenos Aires present a one-sided picture: tango, football, beef, and Parisian architecture. These clichés are part of the city, but they do not do justice to this multi-faceted metropolis.

The people of Buenos Aires like to damn their city when they are there and defend it vehemently when on their travels. No wonder: it is often noisy, dirty, and materialistic, and it forces its residents to take two-hour journeys on buses and subway trains. On the other hand, it is infinitely diverse, modern, and creative. Hardly any other place is so vibrant. Buenos Aires continually reinvents itself and its traditions.

In this book, we introduce you to 111 of the countless facets that make up Buenos Aires – places that can only be discovered at the third or fourth glance and that will surprise even Argentinians. We spent more than a year researching, and criss-crossed the city with cameras for three months. In doing so we were surprised again and again by Buenos Aires, even though we thought we knew it. We would like to share these surprises with you.

¡Que disfruten!

Leonie Friedrich and Benjamin Haas

111 Places

1 The “28 Sport” Shoe Shop

Bowling footwear that lasts forever

It all started in 1928 with prototype 28-A. That, at least, is what the people say who run this shoe shop in Palermo. They see themselves as keeping up the tradition of the Argentinian amateur sportsman Calogero Adinolfi, who, in the 1920s, turned his obsession for good sporting footwear into a business model and made a success of his family company, called 28 Sport. The promise made by his self-appointed successors is: our shoes last forever, because they are made the way shoes were produced in Adinolfi's day, when quality, and not marketing, was the recipe for success.

Ironically, Carlos, Edgardo, and Andrea are not shoe makers but marketing experts. They gave up their jobs with international companies and bought the rights to the 28 Sport brand, which had disappeared from the market for four decades. Their mission was to “save” the quality of the sports shoes of the 1930s, 40s, and 50s. For this purpose they hunted for old shoes on flea markets across Europe. At home, they dissected their discoveries to find out how these miracles of durability were made. Then they persuaded traditional shoe makers in Buenos Aires to bring their old craft back to the light of day.

The result was a range of incomparably robust shoes in an original football, boxing, hockey, or bowling look. There are only 12 pairs of each model in various sizes, and none of them is manufactured again. This concept made 28 Sport the insiders' tip in the retro scene. But they don't really want to be retro. “What we are doing is historical,” they say – using fairly sophisticated marketing language. But they see nothing wrong with that. They describe marketing as an evil that afflicts the world, like climate change. But no matter: their shoes are genuinely unique. It's just that hardly anyone uses them for sports, because these shoes are definitely too heavy for that.

Address Gurruchaga 1481, Palermo, CABA | Getting there Subte B to Malabia or Subte D to Plaza Italia, from each 15 minutes' walk or bus 93 or 142 | Hours Mon–Sat 11:30am–1:30pm & 3–7pm | Tip A few minutes' walk away is busy Plaza Serrano, with a craft market on weekends and lots of pretty cafés and restaurants. Pain et Vin (Gorriti 5132, Tue–Sat noon–10pm, Sun noon–7pm) is especially good.

2 The Academia del Lunfardo

Guardian of the slang of the Río de la Plata

In Argentina, they speak Spanish! Well, not only Spanish, as the Academia del Lunfardo has been proving since 1962. Its role is similar to that of the Academie Française in France and the Real Academia Española in Spain. With one important difference: it is not concerned with standard Spanish, but with a special kind of slang that arose on the Río de la Plata in the last century as a result of a unique moment in society. The ingredients: European immigrants, gauchos, indigenous people, and *porteños*, mixed with an environment of poverty, crime, and the fight to survive in the underclasses of society. This gave birth to Lunfardo, a jargon that was initially belittled by the upper classes as a language for crooks but then inspired the lyrics of tango and went on to conquer all levels of society and provinces of the country.

How about an example? Switching syllables is a famous phenomenon in Lunfardo: gotán stands for tango, and café is turned into feca. Old colloquial expressions from Italian and Portuguese also made their mark on a rich vocabulary that comprises about 6,000 words. The Academia del Lunfardo not only records the language and investigates its origins – it also aims to promote actively a popular culture connected with Lunfardo. For this purpose, it has gathered in its library 4,000 books about the sociolect, the city, and its milieux, as well as some 4,500 tango scores. The academy publishes books and articles, and in the year 2000 established the Day of Lunfardo. Since then, this Argentinian slang, of which not only the people of Buenos Aires are proud, has been celebrated each year on September 5.

Since 1987 the seat of the Academia del Lunfardo has been San Telmo. Between April and December, free concerts and readings are held here on Fridays at 7pm. It is worth attending one of these events, even if you cannot speak Spanish.

Address Estados Unidos 1379, San Telmo, CABA | Getting there Subte C & E to Independencia; bus 39, 53, 60, 96, 102, 126, 129A, or 168 | Hours Mon–Fri 2–7pm, for events see www.lunfardo.org.ar | Tip The Independencia Subte station is well worth seeing thanks to its decoration of tiles in oriental style. You will find information about Arab influences in Buenos Aires on the platforms below.

3 The Agriculture Faculty

Andean atmosphere between skyscrapers

Llamas and alpacas strut gracefully across the highlands of Bolivia and Peru, their typical native countries. And in the Argentinian Andes, too, domesticated species of camel have been known for as long as 5,000 years. But in Buenos Aires, a mere 25 meters above sea level? Anyone who walks for the first time past the campus shared by the faculties of agriculture and veterinary medicine may well be astonished to see llamas craning their necks over the fence by the roadside. This site of those faculties of the Universidad de Buenos Aires is home to more of their kind, as well as all sorts of other domestic animals: donkeys, horses, cattle, geese, and hens. Research is carried out here on animal husbandry, health, and production. There is even a small university clinic for veterinary medicine. Here, in 2012, researchers succeeded in bringing back to life an extinct race of Argentinian alpacas by means of genetic investigations.

A walk across the campus is worthwhile, not only as a brief but free visit to a zoo. Its large park is a popular destination for trippers, especially on weekends. Between lecture theaters and offices, visitors can relax on the lawns to drink mate and enjoy some sunshine. Every other Saturday and Sunday, farmers sell organic products at a big market, and provide advice about healthy eating and organic horticulture.

The main entrance is situated on Avenida San Martín. To the north, the park extends to the other side of the rail tracks. At its end is an intersection with Avenida de los Incas, from where it is only a few *cuadras* to the Parque Chas quarter (see ch. 76). For access to the animals, go a few meters to the right of the main gate. And don't worry: llamas usually only spit at other llamas, as a sign of dominance. If they take aim at humans, it is because they have had unpleasant experiences of them.

Address Av. San Martín 4453, Agronomía, CABA | **Getting there** Main entrance: train on the San Martín line from Retiro to Villa del Parque; bus 47, 57, 78, 105, or 146; side entrance: train on the Urquiza line from Lacroze to Pedro N. Arata | **Hours** Mon–Fri 9am–6pm, dates of the organic market Feria del Productor al Consumidor en la FAUBA on Facebook | **Tip** The Agronomía residential area around the faculties is extremely pleasant, and Julio Cortázar liked it (see ch. 12).

4 Amerika Disco

Wild and colorful nights

Amerika in the Almagro district has been a defining element of the nightlife of Buenos Aires since 1999. The club is a rendezvous for lesbians, gays, bisexuals, transsexuals, and intersexuals, but also for heterosexuals who want to party together until dawn. The only motto is "Be who you are and enjoy it!" When you have paid the admission fee, you can happily leave your wallet in your bag or pocket, as drinks are then free all night.

Electro, house, Latin, and pop are played from Thursday to Sunday on three floors with space for 1,800 people. The atmosphere on the dance floor is always respectfully relaxed – not at all like the scene in other, heterosexual discos in the city, where macho males often set the tone. In the early hours of Saturday and Sunday, a perfectly choreographed transvestite and dance show is performed as the culmination of the weekend party. The crowning glory of this celebration of human diversity is a large tunnel on one of the two galleries. Here everything is allowed that intoxicated night-time sensuality desires. If you are shy about touching, it is better to stay away.

Again and again local residents have tried to take action against Amerika – ostensibly because of its noise. However, a court of law found that there was not too much noise, but that homophobia was the true motivation of the opponents. All in all, it has become easier in recent years for young homosexual Argentinians to come out. The country's Catholic society has become more tolerant, and progressive legislation is bearing fruit. In 2010, Argentina was the first Latin American country to allow homosexuals to marry, giving equal status to gay and lesbian partnerships at all levels. The laws now make reference simply to "married persons," no longer to "man and wife." By this means it has also automatically become legal for married gays and lesbians to adopt children.

Address Gascón 1040, Almagro, CABA | **Getting there** Bus 19, 24, 26, 71, 92, 99, 109, 124, 127, 160, or 168 | **Hours** Fri–Sun, sometimes on Thu and before holidays, midnight–6am; see www.ameri-k.com.ar for the program | **Tip** Three *cuadras* away, the alternative arts center Club Cultural Matienzo is the ideal place to start your evening before going to Amerika (Pringles 1249, Tue–Fri from 7pm, Sat, Sun, & holidays from 8pm).

5 The Antiques Station

Antiques and curiosities by the Tren de la Costa

Buenos Aires and its inhabitants are said to have a tendency to nostalgia. Even if this corresponds to the dream world of the tourist industry more than the actual mood of most people, it is nevertheless astounding to see how many markets, galleries, and shops in the city offer antiques for sale. From the touristy and therefore expensive antiques market in San Telmo to the little stores that lie hidden deep in the shopping galleries of the Microcentro, there is enormous interest in things from past times that have been cleared out of people's households.

The most attractive and out-of-the-ordinary Feria de Antigüedades spreads itself every weekend across the platforms of Station Barrancas in San Isidro in the north of the Provincia. The place itself, with the antiquated appearance of its waiting room, large, ornate station clocks, and the metal bridge that crosses the tracks, seems to be from another era. Since 1997, 70 stands have created a universe of bygone days for collectors, antiques lovers, and all other purchasers of useful and useless things.

At the Feria del Anticuario, porcelain, clocks, glassware, toys, books, lamps, and furniture are piled up as high as the tree tops. Some of the stands specialize in Argentinian country life. Here you will find ploughs, stirrups, and the typical *boleadoras*, a kind of lasso with balls that the gauchos copied from the indigenous people of Patagonia. Other vendors trade in military items, selling objects dating from the two world wars, but also from the wars in Vietnam and the Falkland Islands. Whether you are in search of something particular or simply looking around, you will surely find some rarity or other to take back home.

The trip is rewarding for the journey alone. The Tren de la Costa, a service to which the station belongs, runs along the banks of the Río de la Plata between Vicente López and the Tigre Delta.

Address Station Barrancas (Tren de la Costa), corner of Sebastián Elcano and Perú, Acassuso, San Isidro, Provincia | Getting there Train on the Mitre line from Retiro to Bartolomé Mitre, then change to the Tren de la Costa to Barrancas, or bus 168 toward San Isidro | Hours Sat, Sun, & holidays 10am–7pm | Tip This book takes you to three more strange, hidden places (see ch. 19, 39, & 84) in San Isidro that are only a few minutes' walk from this *feria* – the ideal program for a weekend trip.

6 Atlas and the Old Tree

235 years and still counting

If you stroll across the squares in the center of Buenos Aires, you cannot avoid passing some of the impressively large trees that grow there. They have roots that stick up meters out of the ground and branches as thick as the trunks of other trees. Standing beneath them, we humans look like nothing so much as tiny Lego figures.

This rubber tree is a particularly ancient specimen, the oldest recorded tree in the city. It is said to have been brought from India by a monk. When Recoleta was still a place of fields and meadows outside the city gates, it was planted in 1781 in front of the famous cemetery. The trunk has a diameter of 10 meters, and some of the boughs, with a length of 30 meters, have had to be propped up with steel supports. They reach down almost to the ground and make the tree seem like a huge dome.

You might simply walk on past this green giant, but beneath its canopy of leaves a further attraction is concealed: since October 2014, a branch has been held up by one of the world's strongest men, the legendary Greek titan Atlas. This is a sculpture, entitled *The Atlas of Recoleta*, by the young Uruguayan artist Joaquín Arbiza Brianza, mainly consisting of scrap metal taken from old cars and weighing about 250 kilos. Normally Atlas carries the whole world on his shoulders, but in Recoleta he is supporting a tree that is more than 235 years old.

Since 2006 the old rubber tree has also adorned the official coat of arms of the district of Recoleta. It is the only living witness to the opening of La Biela in 1850, and to this day it provides shade to the terrace of the traditional café. Such famous people as the writers Jorge Luis Borges and Adolfo Bioy Casares used to meet here regularly for a cup of coffee. Two sculptures at one of the tables serve as a reminder of these honored guests, and are a popular photo motif for both tourists and locals.

Address Av. Pres. Manuel Quintana 600, in front of the café La Biela, Recoleta, CABA | **Getting there** Bus 10, 17, 37, 59, 60, 95, 101, 102, 108, 110, or 124 | **Tip** A little way downhill is the Palais de Glace, built in 1911 as an ice rink and now a space for art exhibitions (Posadas 1725, www.palaisdeglace.gob.ar).

7 The Avellaneda Bridges

"To La Boca and back"

This is one of those structures that makes you wish you could travel back in time when you see it. Who would not wish to have experienced the maiden voyage of the Transbordador Nicolás Avellaneda, the old transporter bridge, in 1914?

This harbor bridge, made from steel and copper, once transported pedestrians, horse-drawn carts, cars, and trams across the Riachuelo from the city district of La Boca to Avellaneda in a transporter car measuring 8 by 12 meters. It was operated by cables and pulleys from a small control cabin that can still be seen on the north side. The journey across took half an hour, and ships could pass beneath at all times thanks to the height of the bridge.

"Bridge ferries" of this kind were built in the 19th century, mostly in port cities. This one was made in England and assembled in Buenos Aires by the railway company. In the 1960s it was decommissioned. The number of passengers using the transporter bridge has declined steadily, partly because of a second bridge with a concrete base that was constructed in 1940. This red lifting bridge is only about 100 meters beyond the transporter bridge. Road traffic is interrupted for 10 minutes when large ships pass through. Strangely, it was also named for Nicolás Avellaneda. Presumably the builders realized that it meant the inevitable end for its older sister, and so a replacement was provided for the name, too.

Across the world, only eight transporter bridges remain, several of them still in operation, for example in Middlesbrough, England, on the River Tees, and Newport in Wales. The only remaining transporter bridge in the Americas is the one in Buenos Aires. For some time now, work has been underway to restore it, in the hope of having it included on the UNESCO list of World Heritage Sites. Perhaps a crossing will be possible before time travel is invented.

Address Between Av. Almirante Brown (La Boca, CABA) and J. M. Monatana (Avellaneda, Provincia) | Getting there Bus to the bridges on the La Boca side: 20, 25, 29, 33, 46, 53, 64, 86, 129, 152, 159, 168, or 195; buses 33 and 159 cross the new bridge to Avellaneda | Note In the La Boca district, poverty and lack of prospects have led to a high crime rate. If you don't know your way around here, don't explore on foot. You can easily visit the bridges by bus or taxi. | Hours Viewable from the outside only | Tip The famous Caminito is only a few minutes' walk from here. It is worth looking inside the bar El Samovar de Rasputin, where live concerts are held in the evenings.

8 Avenida Rivadavia

A myth about the world's longest street

When a journalist described Avenida Rivadavia as the longest street in the world in 1914, he was probably still right. It ran from Plaza de Mayo in the historic center of Buenos Aires to Luján, 69 kilometers away. Today this is only a myth that lives on stubbornly. As its name becomes Presidente Perón after 35 kilometers in San Antonio de Padua, it has lost its record-breaking status and joins Western Avenue in Chicago (38 kilometers) and Sunset Boulevard in Los Angeles (35 kilometers) behind the front runner, Yongue Street in Toronto, which heads the global list today at 56 kilometers.

Alongside the 140-meter-wide Avenida 9 de Julio, Avenida Rivadavia remains the city's most important traffic artery. All streets that cross it at right angles change their names here, and the house numbers start again at no. 1. Along it stand some of the city's most important buildings, for example Casa Rosada, the Catedral Metropolitana, and Congress. It is a cross section through the milieux and cultures of the Argentinian capital. Avenida Rivadavia links the contrasts of the city: from the banks and luxurious hotels in the Microcentro to the Jewish quarter of Once, through Barrio Boliviano and out to the poorer suburbs from which thousands of people commute daily to the center.

A recommendation for urban adventurers is to climb up the avenida on foot. Have breakfast on Plaza de Mayo, lunch in Flores, an evening meal in Liniers, beer to round off the day in the Provincia, and take a train back to Once. There is no more impressive way to experience the size of Buenos Aires. You can measure your progress by looking at the house numbers. As every block in Buenos Aires begins at a round hundred, regardless of the number of buildings, you can check how many *cuadras* you have passed. The numbers of the buildings on Avenida Rivadavia end proudly at 27,500.

Getting there Subte line A and the Sarmiento train (from Once) have many stops and more than 100 bus lines go along Avenida Rivadavia for part of their route | **Note** From the Floresta quarter onwards, the avenida passes through some districts with a high crime rate. It is better to avoid these sections after dark or if you are alone. | **Tip** The first president of Argentina, Bernardino Rivadavia, was laid to rest in a mausoleum on Plaza Miserere (also called Plaza Once) on this avenue, which was named for him.

9 Baek-ku

Kimchi and karaoke in the Korean quarter

Korea Town, Pequeña Korea, or Baek-ku – there are many names for the district of the Korean community. The further south you walk on Carabobo from Avenida Rivadavia, the more the street scene changes. Bakeries, supermarkets, beauty salons, doctors, restaurants, churches, and travel agencies – here you find everything in its Korean version. At the schools you can get South Korean leaving certificates, and the menus are printed using the Korean alphabet, even though much has now been translated into Spanish. Most members of the second generation have grown up bilingual.

As a result of the war in their country in the 1950s, the first South Koreans arrived in Buenos Aires in 1965. By the 1990s there were around 45,000 of these immigrants in Argentina, of whom only 15,000 remained after the economic crisis in 2001. Eighty per cent of them live in Buenos Aires today, most of them here in Flores.

For some entertainment with a difference, pay a visit to one of the karaoke bars. 007 has become a hot tip even for outsiders. In its small TV cabins you can find some international pop songs alongside all the Korean hits. "Gangnam Style" is sure to be one of them! And for everyone who has eaten more than enough meat and pasta, the restaurants that offer cuisine from the Far East make a welcome change. Kimchi, the fermented vegetables that are typically Korean, are an essential part of a meal.

Many Koreans live along Avenida Avellaneda, about 10 *cuadras* from the center of Baek-ku. There, on Plaza Angel Gris, stands an important landmark. To celebrate the 200th anniversary of Argentinian independence, the South Korean ambassador inaugurated this replica of a stone pagoda from the Bulguksa Temple. By now everyone is familiar with the Chinatown in Belgrano and its characteristic dragon gate, but by contrast Barrio Coreano is undeservedly overlooked by most people.

Address Monument: Corner of Bogotá and Donato Álvarez. The center of the district is between Avenidas Eva Perón, Castañares, and Carabobo. Karaoke 007: Bacacay 2919, 3rd Floor, all in Flores, CABA | Getting there Subte A to Carabobo, four *cuadras* north of Av. Rivadavia to Plaza Angel Gris or 8–10 *cuadras* south along Carabobo to the heart of the *barrio*; bus to the plaza: 44, 76, 84, 92, 99, 113, 172, or 181 | Note If you don't know your way around, limit your visit to the monument. If you behave inconspicuously (e.g. don't openly carry a camera), you can safely walk along Av. Carabobo. Don't cross Av. Castañares, as here the Villa Miseria Bajo Flores is a place of poverty and crime.

10 The Balcony

Evita and Madonna on the gallery of the Casa Rosada

Madonna is said to have gone to President Menem personally to ask for permission to use the balcony of the presidential palace, the Casa Rosada, as a backdrop for her film *Evita*. Playing the role of Latin America's best-known first lady, she was to sing her version of "Don't Cry for Me Argentina" to the people from there. This was no easy matter: many Argentinians felt sceptical about the project. "Madonna out! Long live Evita!" wrote angry opponents on the walls of buildings. They were afraid that their people's saint, María Eva Duarte de Perón (1919–1952), might be portrayed in the wrong light.

The way they like to see her is closely connected with this balcony. With her husband, Juan Domingo Perón (1895–1974), the "madonna of the shirtless" often stood there to address her supporters. Perón himself used the balcony to stage his appearances in his last three periods in office. You could almost say that the balcony made him president. When he was minister of labor, he carried out a number of social reforms.

This ensured support for him from workers and the poor sections of society, but earned him the disapproval of military leaders. In October 1945, they arrested him. Six days later, hundreds of thousands of supporters gathered in front of the Casa Rosada to demand his release. In this they were successful: at 11pm Perón emerged onto the balcony and spoke to an enthusiastic crowd. This was one of the most significant moments in the history of Argentina. A few months later he was elected president for the first time.

Madonna's wish was granted: in front of 2,000 extras, in 1996 she appeared on the balcony with Jonathan Pryce in the part of Perón. If you look down from it today to Plaza de Mayo, you can sense the vibrant euphoria of the Peronist masses as they hear the voice of Madonna quietly singing "Don't cry for me Argentina. The truth is I never left you …"

Address Casa de Gobierno de la República Argentina (Casa Rosada), Balcarce 50, Monserrat, CABA | **Getting there** Subte A to Plaza de Mayo, Subte E to Bolívar, Subte D to Catedral; bus 7, 22, 28, 33, 50, 56, 91, 103, 130, 143, 152, or 159 | **Hours** Free tours in Spanish: Sat, Sun, & holidays 10am–6pm every 15 minutes; English: 12:30pm & 14:30pm; Portuguese: 1pm & 2:45pm, book in advance: https://visitas.casarosada.gob.ar | **Tip** The Museo Bicentenario is directly connected to the Casa Rosada. For the 200th anniversary of independence it was built on the remains of an old customs house, and is dedicated to the most important moments in the country's history.

11 The Barber La Época

A lively, cultural museum of hairdressing

A visit to the La Época barber is like a journey back in time. In a side street in the down-to-earth Barrio Caballito you will find this strange men's hairdresser, which is also a café, museum, and arts center all in one. The barber, Miguel Ángel Barnes, has been one of the fixtures of the building all his life. He was born and grew up here. In the space now used as a barber's store he ran his mother's little greengrocer's business.

When he opened the barber's store in 1998, his plan was that it would not be like the others. For seven years he collected antique items and made them work again: the old telephone, the piano dating from 1907, and all the relics of the barber's trade from bygone days made his store into something special. Even the outfit of the barbers who work here comes from past times. In La Época you see the origins of the gentleman's hairdresser of the 19th and 20th centuries. The services are for men only. Women are most welcome though – as companions to the men. To enable them to pass the time pleasantly, Miguel has established a café, divided from the hairdressing salon only by a pane of glass. Here you can enjoy excellent coffee and cake in cozy surroundings, between glass cases filled with traditional barber's utensils. As a living museum, the salon has plenty of customers and fully lives up to its name. The National Geographic Society has awarded it the status of unique in the world.

After business hours, events are regularly held in the salon. Alongside talks about the history of the barber's trade, the programme includes jazz and tango. Theater groups, too, use the store as a stage for performances. This mixture of museum, culture, and a heart-warming atmosphere in a small space seems to be Miguel's recipe for success. Regular customers come here from all over the city – if only for a chat over a cup of coffee.

Address Guayaquil 877, Caballito, CABA | **Getting there** Subte A to Primera Junta; bus 2, 5, 25, 36, 42, 49, 52, 53, 55, 84, and others | **Hours** Tue–Fri 9am–2pm & 4–8:30pm, Sat 9am–8pm, events listings on Facebook | **Tip** Walk three *cuadras* south from here Av. del Barco Centenera to see the small Barrio Inglés, built in the English style in 1923 for British railway workers.

12 Barrio Rawson

In the footsteps of Cortázar

Avenida San Martín, Tinogasta, and Zamudio form a small triangle that juts into the site of the Faculty of Agriculture. Although it officially belongs to the Agronomía district, its residents call it Barrio Rawson. A name of its own is justified, as this triangular quarter is clearly different from its surroundings. It has extremely beautiful avenues and a picturesque little plaza at its center. Only a few years after it was built in 1930, its most famous resident lent it literary prestige.

From 1934 Julio Cortázar lived here with his mother and sister in the house at no. 3246 in the street called Artigas. The son of Argentinians, born in Brussels, he came to Buenos Aires in 1918 at the age of four. As a young teacher, he became a master of short stories that lay somewhere between reality and fiction. He took inspiration for his surreal worlds, it is said, here in Barrio Rawson. Indeed, the district is present in many of his texts. It was his final and most important place of residence in Buenos Aires. Even while living in exile in France during the years of Perón's rule, Cortázar never broke free from the city. He returned many times, before dying of leukaemia in 1984 in Paris.

Since those days, hardly anything has changed in Barrio Rawson: the cats that Cortázar described as the "guardians of the sidewalks" still roam peacefully through the streets, and the chattering of sparrows from his story entitled "Omnibus" from the collection *Bestiario*, published in 1951, can still be heard.

Houses are almost never put up for sale here, as they are passed on from generation to generation. Nobody is willing to give up life in this atmosphere, which so inspired one of the most significant Argentinian authors of the 20th century. Pablo Neruda once said these words about the works of Cortázar: "Anyone who doesn't read Cortázar is doomed."

Address Barrio Rawson is bordered by Av. San Martín, Tinogasta, and Zamudio. Cortázar's house: General José G. de Artigas 3246, Agronomía, CABA | **Getting there** Train on the San Martín line from Retiro via Palermo to Villa del Parque; bus 47, 57, 78, 105, or 146 | **Hours** Cortázar's house is viewable from the outside only | **Tip** At the corner of Cortázar and Artigas is the pleasant Café Rayuela, named for one of Cortázar's main novels. The WiFi password is his date of birth (Artigas 3199, Mon–Wed 9am–9pm, Thu–Sun 9am–midnight).

13 The Basilica Clock

The city's first dial hands

Recoleta is one of the most popular and expensive districts in Buenos Aires. Many tourists come here every day to view the city's oldest cemetery and visit the mausoleum of Argentina's famous first lady, Eva Perón. The cemetery is attached to the parish church of Nuestra Señora del Pilar, built in 1732, but was not opened until 90 years later. When you enter the cemetery you automatically walk past the basilica, but most people who come here are unaware of one interesting detail.

To see this feature, look to the right above the entrance at the tip of the small bell gable: the clock. The gable was a typical element of church architecture in the Spanish and Portuguese colonial empires. The idea of crowning it with a clock was, however, far in advance of its time. The clock was made in 1740, and is thus the first and oldest in Buenos Aires. It was the work of the London clockmaker Thomas Windmills, son of Joseph Windmills, who was once the world's most famous clockmaker. Father and son ran a successful company that was employed by the British Crown for, among other contracts, the maintenance of the clock in the Tower of London. The end of this renowned company came in 1743, when Thomas Windmills died.

The face of the timepiece is attached to a ball of cement. Its mechanism consists of normal ropes, which have to be renewed regularly before they wear out. The clockwork is operated to this day by two lead pendulums, each of which is two meters long and weighs 10 kilograms. The clock has to be wound up every 24 hours.

If you visit the museum in the church, you will also have an excellent view of the La Recoleta cemetery and its 4,800 mausoleums. Evita was laid to rest here, along with many deceased Argentinian presidents – though Evita's husband is not among them, as he was buried in the big cemetery in Chacarita (see ch. 26).

Address Junín 1892, Recoleta, CABA | **Getting there** Bus 17, 61, 62, 67, 92, 93, 110, 124, or 130 | **Hours** Check the website for tours; every first or second Sunday in the month at 3pm | **Tip** Down the slope is Plaza Intendente Alvear, better known as Plaza Francia, where one of the most popular craft markets is regularly held on weekends.

14 The Break Club

A destructive therapy session

"Fuck Yoga, Break Stuff." This slogan shouts out in small letters on what used to be a residential building. The unassuming black metal door conceals the first Break Club in Latin America. People come here and pay money to break things, simply so that they can let it all out for once. The slogan states the program. "I'm always so tense in everyday life. Here I can burn off my surplus energy," says a young man waiting for his turn. "It's like therapy, just brilliant," a young couple say afterwards with enthusiasm. They are visibly drenched in sweat following a 30-minute session. While they open a can of beer and collapse on a settee, the young man is invited into the changing room.

A few minutes later he is standing in a plain room with gray concrete walls, wearing protective clothing, and holding a baseball bat. In front of him, as if on an altar, some old computer equipment and a few bottles have been set up. He has paid about $45 to smash them up. Then the door closes, and off he goes. His chosen music booms from the speakers: "Killing in the Name" by Rage Against the Machine.

For regular customers, this ritual takes place often, while for others it is a one-off event. The most expensive package costs approximately $90. "But for that price, two people have fun for up to an hour," says Guido, the founder of the Break Club. And he adds that Argentinians also spend a lot of money on psychologists. This is true. For many of them, a session with their therapist is like a regular check-up at the dentist. Buenos Aires leads the world for its density of psychologists: about 800 per 100,000 inhabitants. In New York, the figure is a mere 100 per 100,000 residents. Most of them work on their own using Freud's dated methods of psychoanalysis. The Break Club may be expensive, but perhaps it is a sensible alternative for some people.

Address Moldes 673, Colegiales, CABA | **Getting there** Mitre train line from Retiro to Colegiales, Subte D to Olleros, bus 41, 44, 59, 63, 66, 67, 68, 80, 113, 152, 168, or 184 | **Hours** Wed–Sun 4–10pm, only by arrangement via www.thebreakclub.com or reservas@thebreakclub.com | **Tip** About 12 *cuadras* away (Paraguay 5499) is Bar Montecarlo, founded in 1922 and one of the last remaining old establishments of its kind in the Palermo district Hollywood (daily 8am–10pm).

15 The Bullet Holes from 1955

Historic scars

Smooth slabs of granite clad the lower parts of the Ministry of Economics on Plaza de Mayo. In one place the stone is full of holes made by a hail of bullets. Immediately in front of this, steps descend to Subte line A. Most people who hurry down them do not notice these historic scars. The holes were heralds of what must be regarded as the most unstable and violent 30 years of Argentinian history.

In the second term of office of Juan Domingo Perón, it was not only the oligarchy of major landowners and the Roman Catholic church that turned against the president, who favored the trade unions. The army, too, had been engaged in a latent conspiracy for years. On June 16, 1955 navy warplanes flew in low to bombard Plaza de Mayo, with the intention of killing Perón in the Casa Rosada. He had been warned, however, and took shelter. The attempted coup turned into a massacre of civilians. The first bomb hit a school bus. A total of 308 people were killed and 800 were injured. The plotters capitulated that same evening. It was the sad baptism of fire of the Argentinian armed forces against their own people.

The marks that were left by this attack on the Ministry of Economics were never removed. Cavallo, a former minister, had a plaque installed in the 1990s above the bullet holes to commemorate the events. From here, if you follow the street Hipólito Yrigoyen a little way downhill, behind the entrance pavilion to the Museo del Bicentenario you will see several bronze faces placed on stakes. This is a work of art dedicated to the victims of the air raid of 1955. In November of that same year a second coup was successful. President Perón fled the country. What followed was three years of military rule that ended in social and political chaos, and ultimately led to the bloodiest dictatorship in Argentinian history, lasting from 1976 to 1983.

Address Plaza de Mayo, Hipólito Yrigoyen 250, Monserrat, CABA | **Getting there** Subte A to Plaza de Mayo, Subte D to Catedral, Subte E to Bolívar; bus 2, 8, 20, 22, 24, 28, 29, 56, 64, 86, and others | **Tip** A short walk away on Av. Alicia Moreau de Justo 980 is the museum ship *Presidente Sarmiento*, a three-masted vessel dating from 1889 that served as a training ship for the Argentinian navy (daily 10am–7pm).

16 Café de García

Picadas and billiards in Villa Devoto

Hugo García can still clearly remember how he once lived in the cramped room behind the kitchen with his parents, brothers, and sisters. Today, it is a room next to the café in which he serves his legendary picadas from Thursday to Saturday. No other eatery in the city has picadas like his.

Picadas are a kind of early-evening meal, usually a plate with chunks of ham, salami, and cheese, eaten when people are feeling somewhat famished in-between meal times. At Café de García, however, picadas are a much more hearty meal than normal: empanadas, fish, olives, vegetable pasties, grilled paprika, and caramelized sausages, to name just a few of the ingredients. If you succeed in eating up all 20 of these diverse tapas, you are guaranteed to feel full the following morning. This is why on picada days the small back room with hunting trophies on the walls is bursting at the seams.

This gourmet orgy is not the only thing that Hugo took over from his parents, Metodio and Carolina García, who founded the café in 1927. The legs of ham above the bar and jumble of decorations are also testimony to the long tradition of the bar. If you take the trouble of making the long trip to Villa Devoto, in this café you will be rewarded with authentic *barrio* atmosphere. Old men read the newspapers or propel billiard balls over the baize tops of the three tables. Every regular has his own cue, which is attached firmly to the wall with a padlock. The grim-looking waiters look as if they have jumped straight out of a 1930s film, and the walls are covered with old enamel advertising signs, as well as photos and autograph cards of the famous people who have honored the café with a visit.

Love of sports is also conspicuous in the café. An item proudly on display is a hand-signed shirt of the legendary footballer Diego Maradona, who lived in Villa Devoto for a time.

Address Sanabria 3302, Villa Devoto, CABA | Getting there San Martín train line from Retiro via Palermo to Devoto, or Subte A to De los Incas, then bus 80 to the corner of Av. Beiró and Sanabria or bus 80, 85, 108, 114, 134, or 146 | Hours Mon–Sat 7–midnight, Thu–Sat special picadas from 6:30pm | Tip Before entering García take a look at the impressive water cistern at the corner of Beiró and Gualeguaychú. Through the windows of this Renaissance-style building of 1917 you can see the tanks.

17_Campanópolis

A fantastic magic village with a medieval look

To take a trip back to the Middle Ages, you don't need a time machine. But you do need a little bit of time, as this place is well off the beaten tourist trail. About 35 kilometers south-west of the city center, covering an area of 200 hectares, lies a magical little village that arose through the imagination of a single man: Campanópolis.

When Antonio Campana was diagnosed with throat cancer in 1983 at the age of 50, he was given 5 years to live. An energetic businessman and millionaire, from that time onward he neglected all his businesses and devoted himself to fulfilling a childhood dream. With the help of 100 workers he began to build his own fairy-tale town – this time with no commercial intentions. Without any previous architectural knowledge but with a great deal of creativity, he designed one building after another. Campana and his people worked 14 hours a day to bring in old paving stones, street signs, and other items, to put them in place and thus in the course of years to make Campanópolis.

"He was a collector, a Messi, an artist with a love of detail!," the tourist guide says enthusiastically. Visitors are shown around the site every Saturday to the sound of medieval music. Steps that lead nowhere, a veranda with no entrance, walls decorated with coins, and doors on the ceiling – Campanópolis is full of unexpected things! Not least because it is so extraordinary, it is often hired as a location for weddings or company events. And it is not surprising to learn that in 2011 the TV channel Latin America presented the new series of *Game of Thrones* here.

More than 40 different buildings, including a train station, a church, and a new town have been constructed over the years – because the doctors didn't get their diagnosis quite right.

Campana lived a further 25 years to dedicate himself to his childhood dream.

Address Bariloche 7300, González Catán, Provincia | **Getting there** Belgrano Sur train line from Estación Buenos Aires to González Catán, then bus 620 (ask the driver to stop near Campanópolis), bus 86 or 96 (ask if the driver is going to González Catán, then to be let out on Ruta 3 at km 30 just before Hospital Simplemente Evita, then walk 12 *cuadras*). Plan enough time for getting there – at least 90 minutes. If you speak no Spanish and don't know the area, go by car or taxi. | **Hours** Sat 9am–1pm by arrangement at www.campanopolis.com.ar (including 90-minute tour in Spanish) | **Tip** You can combine the trip with a visit in the afternoon to the Feria de Mataderos (see ch. 41) or the Torre Espacial (see ch. 107).

18__Cantina Don Chicho

Mamma mia!

Until recently it was still possible to see the grande dame of pasta kneading and rolling out the fusilli herself. Coti Bustamante, the boss at Cantina Don Chicho, is the daughter of Italian immigrants. She took over this traditional pasta restaurant from her father-in-law, Don Chicho, who opened it in 1922. Since then, in the window next to the entrance there has been a table on which the pasta, still made by hand, is visible to guests.

Doña Coti, as she was affectionately known to everyone, died in July 2017. Her descendants are maintaining this culinary heritage, for which she was awarded the title of "guardian of the tradition of Italian migrants" by the city authorities. Italians are by far the largest group of immigrants in Argentina. It is estimated that more than 25 million citizens of the country have at least one Italian ancestor.

The furnishings of the restaurant create that cozy atmosphere that is so typical of simple eateries in Buenos Aires. Diners sit close together at spartan wooden tables covered with paper tablecloths. Football memorabilia covers the walls. The grated Parmesan is served in plastic bowls, and the napkins are sheets torn from a roll of paper towels. Authentic and down-to-earth are the words to describe this cantina, where the decorations consist of football posters and flags. For almost 100 years Don Chicho has been a well-loved place to eat, not only for the Italian community. "Bienvenidos" proclaims the sign on the wall in big letters. The guests take this invitation to heart, and every seat is occupied almost every day of the week. If the 29th of the month happens to be a Sunday, you definitely have to book a table in advance. According to the tradition of "Ñoquis del 29," it is lucky to eat pasta on this day. But whenever you come, don't miss the starter of mixed antipasti and *lengua de ternera*, marinated beef tongue.

Address Plaza 1411, Villa Ortúzar, CABA | **Getting there** Subte B to Tronador – Villa Ortúzar; bus 44, 76, 80, 93, 112, 140, 168, or 176 | **Hours** Tue–Fri from 8:30pm, Sat noon–4pm & from 8:30pm, Sun noon–4pm; bookings at +11/45561463 | **Tip** Only three *cuadras* to the south lies the French bakery L'épi Boulangerie (Roseti 1769, Tue–Sat 7:30am–7:30pm, Sun 9am–1pm).

19 The Carob Tree

Liberate America!

Surrounded by a lush green meadow in San Isidro, Quinta Pueyrredón shines in its whitewash. A gallery consisting of eight columns makes up the façade of this graceful colonial building dating from 1790. You pass through the reception rooms and across a large patio to reach the living rooms, where old furniture and paintings collected by the son of the former owner can be admired. The tour includes a walk in the 1.5-hectare park.

Then suddenly there it is in front of you: a 330-year-old carob tree. At first sight it looks like a large, luxuriantly growing bush. It takes a closer look to make out its shape, with branches that have had so much time to grow that some of them are resting on the ground in more than one place. The whole ensemble has a diameter of 20 meters, and is overgrown with moss and orchids – truly a magnificent specimen. A plaque set into the ground tells of the most important event in its history: "Beneath this historic carob tree, generals San Martín and Pueyrredón decided on the independence of South America."

These generals were among the most important protagonists of the Latin American independence movement in the early 19th century. In the shade of this tree on the quinta that had been Pueyrredón's home since 1815 they are said to have had long discussions about the liberation of South America from Spanish colonial rule. Pueyrredón was a member of the first executive of the United Provinces of Río de la Plata, as Argentina was originally called. The Argentinian soldier San Martín wanted to persuade Pueyrredón that they should liberate Chile and then invade Peru by sea. In 1817 San Martín and his regiment made a spectacular march across the Andes and surprised the Spanish forces in Chile. The rest is history.

If you don't manage to get out to San Isidro, go to Plaza Pueyrredón in Flores to see a carob tree taken as a cutting from this one.

Address Rivera Indarte 48, Acassuso, San Isidro, Provincia | **Getting there** Mitre train from Retiro toward Mitre to Olivos, change to Tren de la Costa to San Isidro, or Mitre train toward Tigre to San Isidro, then walk 10 minutes toward the river; bus 168 toward San Isidro | **Hours** Mar–Oct Tue & Thu 10am–6pm, Sat & Sun 2–6pm, Nov–Feb 3–7pm, for events see www.museopueyrredon.org.ar | **Tip** Ten minutes' walk north along the tracks, hidden away in San Isidro R station, is a rugby museum, devoted to the history of a sport that is extremely popular in Argentina (Juan B. de Lasalle 653, Tue–Sun 10am–6pm).

20 Casa de las Empanadas

42 culinary treats

Empanadas, pasties with a filling, are a between-meals snack in Argentina. They are most popular, ordered by the dozen, on Sundays, when people don't want to cook for themselves. In Buenos Aires almost everyone has a favorite empanada store. There are large chains with branches in every district of the city, but also traditional family bakeries that continue to have loyal customers. The usual fillings are minced beef, chicken, or ham and cheese. Of course, there are differences in quality, but they are sometimes a matter of taste. Some prefer them to be deep fried, while others like their empanada best when it has been baked in an oven.

Casa de las Empanadas in Saavedra, well off the beaten tourist track, surpasses all others. Since 1991 it has been producing the best pastry and an unrivalled variety of fillings. The owner, Oscar Rolon, has served more than 40 different *gustos* (flavors) here. Alongside 10 varieties with meat, cut and seasoned in various ways, he has created his own flavors: chicken with blue cheese, aubergine with bell pepper and tomato, or sausage with Italian provolone cheese and onions. The date-and-bacon filling has clearly been borrowed from Spanish tapas. Those who like it hot opt for the versions labeled "picante." In Casa de las Empanadas you can then be certain that you will get something spicy – and this cannot otherwise be taken for granted in Argentina. Treats for dessert are vanilla apple with raisins and dulce de leche, the ultra-sweet caramel cream that is typical of Latin America.

The store with its plain furnishings is basically for the delivery service, and therefore has no tables. When the weather is good, the best place to eat the empanadas is therefore Parque Saavedra, one of the oldest parks in the city: from Casa de las Empanadas first cross the rail tracks and then walk five *cuadras* along Av. García del Río.

Address Av. Dr. R. Balbín 4045, Saavedra, CABA | Getting there Mitre train line from Retiro toward Mitre to L. M. Saavedra; you can also catch the train at Station Carranza in Palermo (Av. Santa Fé / Av. Cabildo); bus 29, 41, 67, 71, 93, 110, or 130 | Hours Daily except Tue 10am–11pm, Sun 10am–3pm & 7–11pm; orders for local delivery at +11/45421650 | Tip If you take the Mitre train from Retiro and the Tren de la Costa to San Isidro, you automatically pass by. A trip to places no. 5, 37, 53, and 84 in this book can easily be combined with a visit to La Casa de las Empanadas.

21 Casa de las Murgas

Carnaval porteño

Murga stands for a kind of music and its performance, on the one hand, and for the musicians' groups on the other hand. Various myths surround the origins of this popular custom. The tradition probably came from Spain and was adapted in various South American countries, where it is usually practiced at carnival time. The music of slaves is said to have made its mark on this style. Big drums and cymbals, satirical songs, and colorful costumes are the main pillars of *murga porteña*.

Oscar Schuhmacher has been captivated by a love of murga that began in his youth. The depot in which members of his group used to store their instruments developed into the Casa de las Murgas from 2002 onwards. The small premises serve as a workshop, a store, a meeting place, and a museum all at the same time. Here Oscar began to sell pipes, sticks, gloves, and fabrics for the costumes at low prices. Today, he makes drums himself, helps people to record CDs, and collects photographs and specialist literature. He does repairs, gives advice, sources items, and lives for murga, the passion of his life. Over the years, the Casa de las Murgas turned into something like the collective memory of *carnaval porteño* and its special music. Here you can investigate its mysterious roots and philosophize about it with Oscar for hours. He uses emotional expressions when he talks about murga: bohemia, marginalization, pride, and identity. For murgeros, their own *barrio* is extremely important. Almost every group takes the name of its district. Los Herederos de Palermo is the name of Oscar's murga.

Today, you can find the drums at sports stadiums and political demonstrations. But if you want to get an impression of what it is truly like, go to a murga spectacle. Now they take place not only at carnival time, but all year round. Most of them are announced on the Facebook page of Casa de las Murgas.

Address Juan Ramírez de Velasco 530, Villa Crespo, CABA | **Getting there** Subte B to Malabia – Osvaldo Pugliese; bus 15, 19, 55, 57, 71, 106, 109, 110, 127, 141, or 168 | **Hours** Mon – Fri 4 – 9pm | **Tip** At the corner of Av. Corrientes and Julián Álvarez, three *cuadras* away, is the old pharmacy Del Águila, dating from 1895. Farmacia de la Estrella (see ch. 40) may be 61 years older, but it is worth taking a look at Del Águila.

22 Casa de los Leones

Beware – it bites!

The lion has taken a firm hold of the young man. With one paw it is pressing him to the ground, while baring its teeth with relish. The victim is trying to shield himself with one arm, but it is clear that his situation is hopeless. This marble statue impressively illustrates what, according to a legend, happened here more than 100 years ago.

Casa de los Leones, a magnificent villa in the district now called Barracas, belonged to a millionaire businessman, Eustoquio Díaz Vélez, from 1880. He liked to invest in the trade in exotic animals, and in his private life preferred to be surrounded by real lions than by domestic cats. This passion was to be his undoing.

When his daughter celebrated her engagement in the park of the villa, the big cats were in their cages – all except one. A lion had escaped, and came to join the party. The guests froze in fright. Only Díaz Vélez reacted promptly, rushing into his house. He grabbed a rifle and shot the lion from a window, but he was too late, as his future son-in-law had already been mauled by the beast. Was this a coincidence, or was the lion jealous? Whatever the truth, the incident had dramatic consequences: in despair at the loss of her fiancé, Díaz Vélez's daughter committed suicide.

Her father replaced all the lions with the statues that still adorn the park today. Even from the great gates at the entrance, stone cats gaze down at passers-by. It is not known why Eustoquio Díaz Vélez decided to commemorate the dreadful events of that afternoon with one of the statues. The legend does not tell us all the details. It is said, however, that the ghosts of his daughter and her beloved still haunt Casa de los Leones.

Since 1965 the house has been an institution serving people with handicaps. Today the statues cannot therefore be seen from close up, but only by looking through the garden gate.

Address Av. Manuel Montes de Oca 110, Barracas, CABA | **Getting there** Subte C to Constitución; bus 4, 9, 10, 12, 17, 28, 39, 45, 46, 51, and others | **Tip** Next door is the children's hospital, Dr. Pedro de Elizalde, established in 1779. It was the first pediatric clinic in the Americas, housed in an impressive building.

23_Casa del Teatro

A retirement home for penniless artists

At the end of a long and glittering life in the limelight, actors and other artists whose income is too small to support them can find refuge in the Casa del Teatro. This institution in the city center, which opened in 1938, was founded by Regina Pacini (1871–1965), a former first lady and soprano. Her model was a retirement home for impoverished opera singers that Giuseppe Verdi had established more than 30 years before in Milan. Several generations of actors have spent the autumn of their lives in the Casa del Teatro. Today the 10-story building is occupied by about 35 former stars of the local theater and music scene. In addition to a room they receive full board and medical care free of charge.

It is not only the fine Art Deco façade that makes a visit to the Casa del Teatro worthwhile. Alongside a small chapel, it has a theater auditorium, a public library specializing in the performing arts, and a boutique selling second-hand clothing that has been donated by well-known artists. Here you can find elegant evening dresses with sequins that once sparkled on the city's stages. The Casa del Teatro also accommodates two small rooms with museum exhibits. One of them is dedicated to the founder of the institution, the other to the tango legend Carlos Gardel.

With luck you might encounter the president of the foundation, Linda Peretz. A woman of a certain age, an actor herself since she was young, she always has a smile on her lips and fits perfectly in this setting of glamorous urban ladies. She has gained the affection of the well-known residents of the Casa del Teatro: "I'm like their mother," she says – being about 15 years younger than most of her charges. She organizes excursions and, something that is particularly close to her heart, "shows" in which the residents perform. "They are stars, and should be able to feel like that even at an advanced age."

Address Av. Santa Fe 1243, Retiro, CABA, www.casadelteatro.org.ar | Getting there Subte C to San Martín, or Subte D to Tribunales; bus 10, 12, 29, 37, 39, 59, 60, 75, 99, 101, and others | Hours Mon–Sat 2–6pm | Tip Only a few *cuadras* along Avenida 9 de Julio is Parque San Martín, with its big monument to the eponymous liberator, a monument with an eternal flame for Argentinians who fell in the Malvinas/Falklands War, and the Le Doute sculpture (see ch. 60).

24_Casa por la Identidad

Do you know who you are?

In November 2015 Mario Bravo found out that he was not the person he thought he was. For 38 years he believed that the wrong people were his parents. He is one of the children who were taken from their mothers during the military dictatorship of the years 1976 to 1983 before their mothers were murdered. Since 1977 the grandmothers have been campaigning for the fates of their vanished children and grandchildren to be established. The "madres" and "abuelas de la Plaza de Mayo" became world-famous for this. Thanks to their help, Bravo found his mother again. She was one of the few to survive imprisonment. Today, more than 400 people in Argentina are living with a false identity.

The Casa por la Identidad is dedicated to these stolen grandchildren. Its home is the former school for mechanics of the Argentinian navy (ESMA), in which some 5,000 left-wing opponents of the regime and guerilleros were tortured and later killed in a secret prison during the years of dictatorship. It is said that only 200 people left ESMA alive. It is just a stone's throw from the stadium in which the final of the football World Cup was held, at the same time, in 1978. President Menem wanted to demolish the military buildings in the 1990s, but massive resistance from human rights organizations prevented this. In 2007 President Néstor Kirchner decided to preserve the "ex ESMA" as a place of commemoration, and handed over one of the buildings to the grandmothers.

A photo exhibition covering 5,200 square meters tells the story of the abuelas and the grandchildren who have been found. The methods of genetic science used for the search are explained. The quotes from those who rediscovered their true identity are most impressive. On a wall of the entrance is a small number: 117. It denotes the latest status of how many grandchildren have been found. Look at the number when you visit: is it higher now?

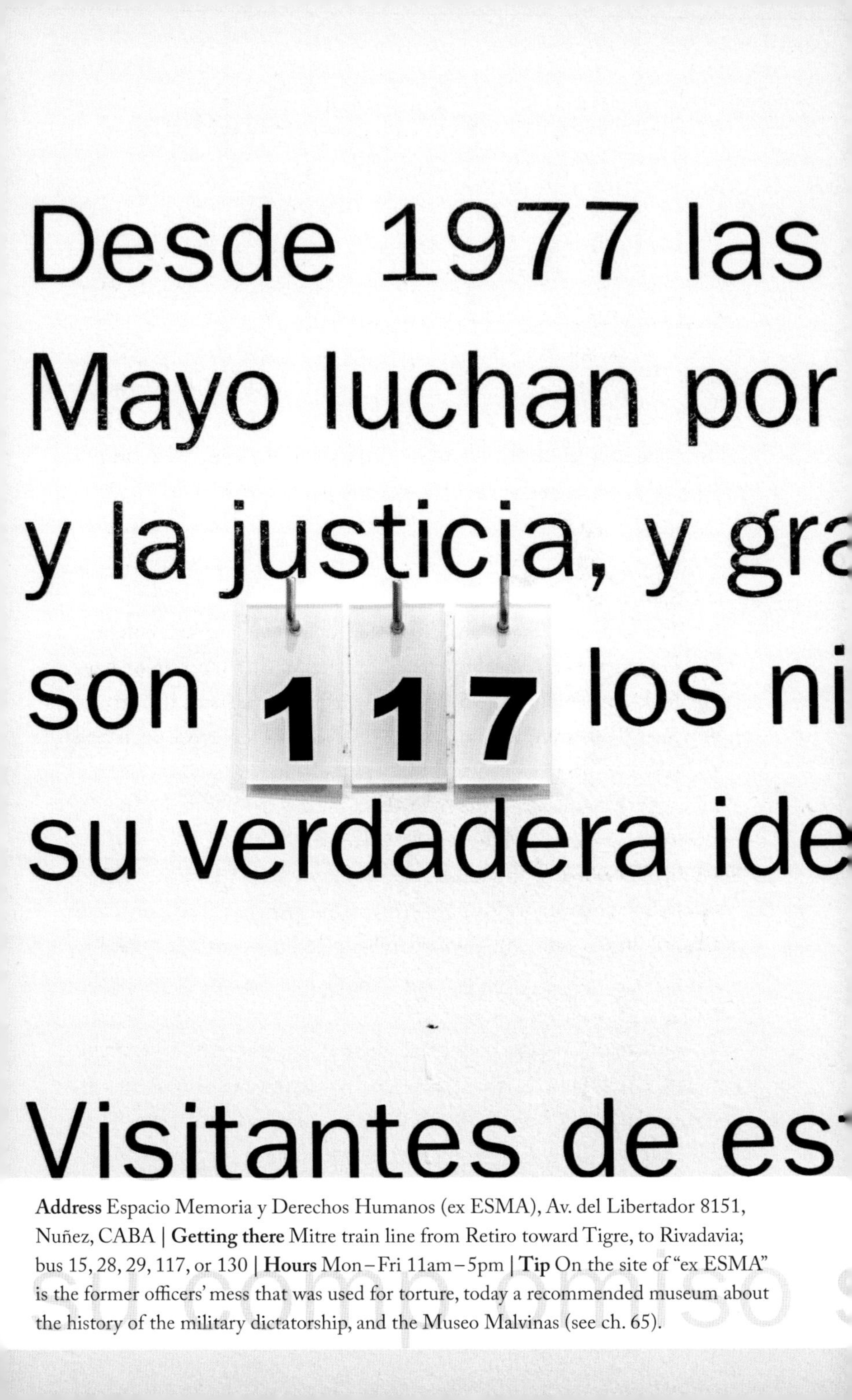

Address Espacio Memoria y Derechos Humanos (ex ESMA), Av. del Libertador 8151, Nuñez, CABA | **Getting there** Mitre train line from Retiro toward Tigre, to Rivadavia; bus 15, 28, 29, 117, or 130 | **Hours** Mon–Fri 11am–5pm | **Tip** On the site of "ex ESMA" is the former officers' mess that was used for torture, today a recommended museum about the history of the military dictatorship, and the Museo Malvinas (see ch. 65).

25 Casino Puerto Madero

A floating political game

Gambling is prohibited in Buenos Aires. Nevertheless, there is an imposing casino in Puerto Madero – and it is perfectly legal. How can this be?

In 1999, the Argentinian government got the better of the city and its mayor, Fernando de la Rúa. Through the national lottery, it announced the opening of a casino that would float on the waters of the Río de la Plata. The trick was that the river belongs to the nation and is therefore not subject to the jurisdiction of the city authorities. De la Rúa was angry. He took the case to the courts of law. The newspaper *La Nación* accused the government of ruining the morals of the country and leading the poor sections of the population into temptations that would mean their final ruin.

However, the political game ran its course. The concession was given to a Spanish company, and the casino ship opened for business on October 8, 1999 in the middle of all the legal wrangling. It had been built in 1995 in New Orleans and is a replica of the famous casino steamships that plied the waters of the Mississippi in the late 19th century – a real eye-catcher. Because of the legal disputes, it initially had to be moored in Uruguay. There it was registered under the Argentinian flag and named *Estrella de la Fortuna*, star of fortune. A few days later this lucky star sailed into the docks of Puerto Madero, which are admittedly within the municipal boundaries, but are filled with national river water. The 1,300 parking spaces and a large lobby with restaurants are situated on dry land, but the one-armed bandits are crammed together on the crowded decks. In 2006 a second ship, the *Princess*, was moored.

In one respect, however, the floating casino was forced to comply with national navigation laws: it has a captain, a ship's engineer and an entire crew – even though it never weighs anchor and moves away. Ahoy!

Address Av. Elvira Rawson de Dellepiane, Dársena Sur, Puerto Madero, CABA | Getting there Free minibus shuttle from the corner of Av. Córdoba and Leandro N. Alem (24 hours a day) and from Av. Rivadavia and Lima (3pm–1:30am); bus 4, 20, 25, 33, 61, 62, 64, 86, 93, 129, and others | Hours Open daily 24 hours | Tip Take Av. Elvira Rawson 700 meters north to the impressive Nereids Fountain, made in 1903 by an Argentinian sculptor. The work was originally intended to stand on Plaza de Mayo.

26 The Chacarita Cemetery

A walk through the necropolis

The cemetery in Recoleta is without doubt one of the most popular sights in Buenos Aires. Every day it draws hundreds and hundreds of tourists, who come to see 4,780 mausoleums of wealthy and famous people. On a website for tourist rankings, this magnet for visitors even took eighth place out of 803 activities in Buenos Aires at the end of 2017.

The Cementerio de la Chacarita gets much less attention, although it possesses several fascinating sights. Due to the sheer size of this necropolis (95 hectares, about 135 football pitches), simply walking across it is an experience in itself. The mausoleums are divided into districts, and you can take a taxi on the numbered roads direct to the tomb that you are looking for. There are also imposing pantheons of various organizations, for example that of the Spanish Society. The federal police have their own area, and you can also find a British and a German section.

Don't miss the grave of the Argentinian tango legend Carlos Gardel (1890–1935) at the intersection 6/33. Fans like to put a burning cigarette in the hand of his statue. This is said to keep his spirit alive. Further famous people who are buried in this cemetery include President Juan Domingo Perón (1895–1974), the aviation pioneer Amalia C. Figueredo (1895–1985), and Hans Langsdorff (1894–1939). The last-named was the captain of the German pocket battleship *Admiral Graf Spee*, which was scuttled by its own crew in 1939 off the coast of Uruguay following an engagement with three ships of the Royal Navy. But that is a different story.

The cemetery was laid out in 1871 after an outbreak of yellow fever, as the burial ground in Recoleta was no longer large enough. There was even a funeral tram for transporting coffins from the city center. By the way, in the rankings on the tourist website, the Cementerio de la Chacarita is in 153th place, and is clearly a well-kept secret.

Address The cemetery has many entrances; the main entrance is on Av. Guzmán 680, Chacarita, CABA | Getting there San Martín train from Retiro and Palermo to La Paternal, or Subte B to Lacroze; bus 4, 42, 44, 47, 63, 65, 71, 78, 111, 123, or 127 | Hours Daily 7:30am–5pm, guided tours in Spanish every 2nd and 4th Sat of the month at 10am (except when it rains) | Tip Opposite the main entrance is a traditional pizzeria, Imperio (corner of Av. Lacroze and Av. Corrientes, Sun–Fri 5am–midnight, Sat round the clock). It serves typical Argentinian pizza with a thick base and lots of cheese.

27 The Chalet at Av. 9 de Julio

Siesta above the clouds

This family home has no more than three stories but is the tallest in the city. If you see it by chance, you will be amazed. How did it get on the roof terrace of a nine-story building on Avenida 9 de Julio? Rafael Díaz, an immigrant from Valencia, once earned a fortune here with his furniture store – the largest showroom of its kind in Latin America. He was the first person in Argentina to sell furniture from a catalog with payment by instalments. The story goes that this millionaire wanted to have a good place to take his siesta. In those days, the afternoon nap lasted from 1pm until 4pm. As his home was far outside the city in the Provincia, in 1927 he simply built a little house on top of his furniture store – right on the roof terrace, next to the displays of garden furnishings.

Back in those days, neither the obelisks nor the 14-lane Avenida 9 de Julio existed. And when it was constructed in 1937, there was an open view of the chalet, because a whole row of housing blocks had been pulled down to make way for the new showcase boulevard. The result was a perfect example of free marketing. Díaz and his little house were illustrated on many postcards without making any effort, and the radio jingle "Díaz. The furniture store with the chalecito" was in every ear. It was broadcast by the store's own radio station.

Rafael Díaz died in 1968, and his store had to close down in the 1970s. The chalet suffered many years of neglect. Then it became home to a fashion agency and a photographic lab. Today, it houses offices, which still belong to the great-granddaughter of Díaz. Nowadays, however, hardly anyone stops to point out what used to be a famous house up in the clouds. No wonder – it has been swallowed up in the jungle of office blocks and huge illuminated advertisements. There are only a few angles of view from which you can see the chalet clearly.

Address Sarmiento 1113, San Nicolás, CABA | **Getting there** Subte B to Carlos Pellegrini, Subte C to Diagonal Norte, Subte D to 9 de Julio; bus 6, 22, 24, 26, 28, 29, 33, 50, 56, 61, and others | **Hours** Viewable from the outside only | **Tip** You can see the chalet from various viewing points in the city center, for example from Galería Güemes (Florida 165 / San Martín 170, Mon–Fri 3–5:40pm, tour every 20 minutes, for pre-booked groups also in the mornings).

28 The Church Door

The kiss of Judas from the angel of death

It is a peculiar feeling to stand in front of this church door if you know what happened here. The case of the Iglesia Santa Cruz shows with particular clarity how unscrupulously the military regime of General Videla proceeded against the opposition between 1976 and 1983. Some 30,000 people disappeared during those years.

The Catholic Church played an inglorious part in this period. Many bishops shared the military regime's view of who the enemy was: communism. The majority silently accepted what then happened, and some actively supported the regime. The Church of Santa Cruz was an exception. It joined the resistance movement against state terrorism and was a place of refuge for relatives of the people who disappeared, including the founders of the Madres de la Plaza de Mayo.

One person who attended the meetings was Gustavo Niño, who claimed that his brother had disappeared. This blond young man, inconspicuous and popular, was in fact the spy Alfredo Astiz. He specialized in infiltrating civil protest groups. When the decision was taken in December 1977 to abduct the human rights group from the Iglesia Santa Cruz, he was their angel of death. Those who were to be taken away were kissed on the cheek by Astiz beneath the arch of the church entrance – 12 of them. It was the fatal signal given to his accomplices. Several of the bodies were found later and buried in the nave of the church. The case gained international publicity, because the victims included two French nuns.

Thanks to the amnesty laws of the 1990s, Astiz was able to continue his service in the armed forces. When the laws were annulled, he was sentenced to life imprisonment in 2011 and 2017. This church entrance was the setting for a real kiss of Judas: "Now he that betrayed him gave them a sign, saying, Whomsoever I shall kiss, that same is he: hold him fast." (Matthew 26: 48).

Address Corner of Estados Unidos and General Urquiza, San Cristóbal, CABA | Getting there Subte E to Urquiza; bus 23, 88, or 115 | Hours During daytime and for Mass | Tip On Plaza Mariano Boedo two *cuadras* to the west stood the tram station La Capital, from where the first electric tram departed for Flores. Parts of the station, built in 1897 and closed in 1962, survive.

29 Choripan on the Costanera

Fish and chips for Brits, burgers for Americans

… and choripan for the Argentinians! A sausage in a baguette is the perfect snack to eat between meals or on the hoof. It is easy to make, quickly consumed, and cheap. Originally an appetizer for an Argentinian *asado*, a traditional barbecue, the spicy sausage has gained its own reputation and is now on sale all over the country, often as a main course served in bread, and for preference in snack bars by the roadside.

On the Costanera, the coastal road that runs along the Río de la Plata, chori shacks have been set up every 50 meters and try to out-do their neighbors. They serve not only the grilled sausages, seasoned with fennel, nutmeg, paprika, cinnamon, and cloves, but also hamburgers, *bandiola*, and *churrasquito*. During daylight hours there is no better place close to the center with such a clear view of the river. On sunny days, people take a midday break with their colleagues here, and travelers fill up before their flights, as the municipal airport is nearby. As most of the stalls are open 24 hours a day, they are popular with people who have been out dancing all night. Unless you are a vegetarian, a meal of choripan on the Costanera road is not to be missed. And one detail is an essential part of the experience: chimichurri, an oily paste made from parsley, pepper, and oregano.

Each year, 600 million choripanes are devoured in Argentina. This national dish is also popular in the neighboring countries of Paraguay, Chile, and Uruguay, and has also become a continent-wide fast-food delicacy, known as far away as Columbia. By the way: choripan is an acronym, formed from the words chorizo and pan – which mean, respectively, sausage and bread. The Argentinian version of the hot dog, which is also famous but does not taste quite so good, is pancho, a name that uses the same play on words – but the other way round!

Address Av. Costanera Rafael Obligado, Palermo, CABA (near the domestic airport Aeroparque Jorge Newbery), e.g. El Taño Criollo | **Getting there** Bus 33, 45, or 160 | **Hours** Daily, 24 hours | **Tip** On a trip to the Costanera, stop in at the Club de Pescadores, a magical-looking, 100-year-old fishermen's club.

30_Club de Tango

A treasury for the feeling that you can dance

This cornucopia of tango culture gets no passing trade. It is well hidden on the fifth floor of an office block, not far from the Congress building. The porter is pleased to tell you whether Hilda Saigg, the proprietor of the Club de Tango, is in the building. She is an elderly lady who comes, in principle, every afternoon, except when she has to go to the doctor or has family commitments.

Since the death of her husband, Oscar Himschoot, in 2005, she has run the place, which is always packed, on her own. Even though the opening hours are not as long as in the past, you can be sure to find a wide assortment of tango rarities here: original music scores, videos, postcards, posters, magazines, and of course great quantities of CDs by Argentinian tango bands.

The intention was merely that these premises would house the editorial team of a small magazine that Oscar published under the name *Club de Tango*. He gave up his work as a businessman and dedicated himself from that time entirely to tango, his great passion. The journal quickly became a well-loved publication for insiders, but he could not live from this income alone. That is why the small editorial space in office number 114 was extended and made into a tango store. Since then, dancers and tango lovers from all over the world have come to the club to stock up on the latest music, to search for an old issue of the magazine, or simply to chat about last night's *milonga*.

Hilda no longer dances herself. "When you have always danced with the same partner for so many years, you no longer want to adapt," she says. What will happen to the store when she is no longer alive? That is something that no one wants to contemplate. Her children and grandchildren help with the website and the overseas mail-order business, "but nobody will take this place over," Hilda assumes. It would be a shame to lose this little gem!

Address Edificio Rose Marie, Paraná 123, 5th floor, office no. 114, San Nicolás, CABA | **Getting there** Subte A to Sáenz Peña, Subte B to Uruguay; bus 6, 7, 9, 10, 17, 24, 26, 29, 45, 50, and others | **Hours** Mon–Fri noon–5pm, but phone in advance to be sure: +11/43727251 | **Tip** Around Congress are more hidden places that this book features: the Barolo Palace (see ch. 73), Pasaje Rodolfo Rivarola (see ch. 78), and the university and café Madres de la Plaza de Mayo (see ch. 94).

31 Conventillo de la Paloma

Lonely testimony to mass immigration

In 1914 half of the population of Buenos Aires had come from abroad. Thousands of the immigrants who had been attracted to Argentina were accommodated in shared housing, places that were named *conventillos* after the cramped cells of monks. Nationalities and dialects, professions, and ideas came together here. This was fertile soil for the growth of the *cultura popular* that was expressed in tango and Lunfardo, the regional idiom.

Some 400 immigrants from Europe lived in the 112 rooms of the Conventillo de la Paloma. It was built in 1886 for workers at a shoe factory, La Nacional de Calzados. Each room had its own cooking facilities, but with only two bathrooms for the whole building, the hygienic situation was dreadful.

Today, only 17 families live here, most of them of Argentinian origin. They are campaigning to have this historic building declared a heritage monument, because the heirs of the factory owners have laid claim to the site since 2011 and want to demolish the *conventillo*. Abel Acosta, spokesman for the community of residents, would like to establish an arts center with a museum here. This is justified, because among the structures of this kind that testify to the mass immigration of the 19th century, the *conventillo* is one of the last to survive in good condition.

This *conventillo* owes its name to the legendary figure of La Paloma, a lady in a white dress. Some say she was a worker, others maintain she was a prostitute. Whichever is right, the men of the *conventillo* are said to have thrown themselves at her feet when she descended the stairs from her small balcony in the room at the end of the corridor. In 1929, a play dedicated to her was premiered, and to this day it is regularly performed on stage. Abel is pleased to give guests a tour of the *conventillo* and show them La Paloma's balcony, which now belongs to his own patio.

Address Serrano 156, Villa Crespo, CABA | **Getting there** San Martín train line from Retiro to Chacarita, Subte B to Malabia; bus 15, 24, 34, 42, 55, 57, 76, 106, 109, 110, 112, or 166 | **Hours** Accessible 24 hours, but from the outside only; you are most likely to meet Abel on weekends from 11am–5pm; or make an appointment via lapalomaconventillo@gmail.com or +11/48579161 | **Tip** The tourist attraction El Caminito in the La Boca harbor quarter consists of former conventillos. They have been smartened up for visitors and now house souvenir stores instead of families.

32 Convento de Santo Domingo

Signs of battle and war trophies

The usual fittings of Roman Catholic churches include images of the Virgin Mary, colorful stained-glass windows, confessionals, and religious paintings. War trophies, by contrast, make for an unusual interior. However, in the passages around the main altar of the Convento de Santo Domingo there hang four such trophies, in the form of faded and tattered Union Jacks.

The banners were captured by General Santiago de Liniers when his unit successfully repulsed the first British attempt to invade Buenos Aires in 1806. Before he set off to join battle, General Liniers took part in a Mass in this basilica and prayed to the Virgin Mary of the Rosary to stand by him. In return for her support, he promised to donate the British flags if he were victorious. The conversation that Liniers held with a priest in relation to this promise is documented in the church records. Liniers was as good as his word. On August 12, 1806 he defeated forces of the British navy, and on August 24 he handed over the captured flags to the convent, where they have been carefully preserved to this day, behind glass and framed.

When Britain again tried to conquer the city a year later, the convent played a key part in the fighting for the second time. Invaders took up position on the east tower of the basilica, and a unit of the militia fired cannon at them. The tower was severely damaged, and many of the cannonballs remained wedged in the walls. This conflict went down in history as the Battle of Santo Domingo. During President Rosas' period of office, between 1835 and 1852, the cannonballs were removed, but to commemorate these glorious events they were replaced with wooden replicas. They can still be seen in the façade of the tower. As it has been thoroughly restored, most people either do not notice them or take them to be some kind of strange adornment.

Address Av. Belgrano 422, at the corner of Defensa, Monserrat, CABA | Getting there Subte E to Belgrano; bus 22, 24, 28, 29, 86, or 126 | Hours During Mass; tours by arrangement: +11/43311668 | Tip A fitting accompaniment to the history of this church is a visit to the Jesuit tunnels on Manzana de las Luces (ch. 52).

33__The Cromañón Memorial

Shoes and graffiti commemorate 194 victims

This is simultaneously a place of memorial and of protest. Right behind Once station, graffiti, hand-written notes, and flowers commemorate the victims of a severe fire on the night of December 30, 2004 in a club called República Cromañón. During a concert of the rock band Callejeros, someone in the audience set off a firework – at that time, nothing unusual in the enthusiastic celebration of concerts. However, before long the ceiling cladding caught fire, the lights went out, and panic broke out among the audience. Almost 200 people were killed by toxic fumes or were crushed to death. As this happened just before New Year's Eve, which is traditionally a family celebration, many of the victims were related.

The tragedy had far-reaching political and social consequences. The mayor of Buenos Aires was suspended, suspected of corruption in the award of the license to the club owners. The latter were sentenced to 20 years' imprisonment in 2009, as 3,200 people were crammed into a club that was only licensed for 1,200. Even worse, most of the exits were locked. Members of the band, who were also involved in the organisation, were also prosecuted for causing death by negligence, but found not guilty. The government then tightened up the safety laws for bars and clubs immensely, which led to many closures. All over Argentina, people referred to this as the "Cromañón effect."

Here, only one block from the site of the tragedy, relatives of the victims come to this day to express their grief and their anger: "End the impunity" and "Cromañón never again!" for example, say the protest notes on the walls. The shoes of the deceased, salvaged from the ruins, became a symbol of Cromañón.

On the tenth anniversary of the disaster, the area in front of the club was turned into a pedestrian zone and officially recognized as a place of memorial.

Address Plaza Miserere, corner of Bartolomé Mitre and Ecuador, Balvanera; the ruin of the disco: Bartolomé Mitre 3070 | **Getting there** Subte H to Once, or Subte A to Plaza Miserere; bus 5, 7, 8, 19, 31, 32, 41, 61, 62, 64, and others | **Tip** On the other side of the tracks is KONEX (Sarmiento 3131), an arts center on the site of a disused factory, where Bomba de Tiempo, a huge percussion band guaranteed to get your feet tapping, play every Monday at 7pm.

34 Don Luis' Carousel

Where grandma and grandpa once went round and round

There are children's carousels all over the city. La Calesita de Don Luis is one of the oldest and most delightful of them. It does not stand on a fairground or a playground like most of the others – its circular pavilion peeps out over the wall of a tiny patio. Until his death in 2013 at the age of 93, it was operated there by Luis Rodríguez, who had taken it over from his father. Don Luis always had a smile on his lips and sweets for his young customers, but had no children himself, so his godchild José Luis, the son of a cousin, inherited the family heirloom. Every weekend, José Luis makes the carousel go round and round again for the children of the *barrio*. In the past he had enjoyed helping Don Luis, but his "real-life" job is to fit cars with gas-powered engines.

The father of Don Luis bought the fairground ride in 1920 and took it around Buenos Aires from one fair to another. Back in those days, it had one horsepower – with a living source of traction. The horse started to trot as soon as it heard the sound of the little fairground organ. In 1965, when he had to look after his mother, Don Luis decided to install the *calesita* once and for all in his yard. He was forced to reduce its size a little, but was thus able to set up the only children's attraction of this kind that stands on the premises of a private house.

The wooden horses and airplanes are the originals, which makes them 100 years old. But most of all, the children like to ride on a giraffe or a camel that Don Luis made himself. Today, children are brought here by their grandparents, who once went round in circles themselves on these figures, beaming with joy. "The best way to commemorate Don Luis is also to keep the carousel going," says his godchild José. But the old man is honored in another way: every year on November 4, the birthday of Don Luis, the day of the carousel is celebrated.

Address Corner of Ramón Falcón and Miralla, Liniers, CABA, www.facebook.com/calesitadonluis | Getting there Sarmiento train line from Once to Villa Luro, then about 10 minutes' walk, or Subte A to San Pedrito, and then bus 8, 86, 88, 96, 104, 136, or 163 | Hours Fri–Sun, irregularly on Thu and public holidays from 5:30pm | Tip You can combine a visit with a previous trip to the Parque Avellaneda (see ch. 75), which is only a few minutes away by taxi or bus (seven *cuadras* walk to Av. Rivadavia, then bus 1, 2, 8, 86, 88, 96, 104, 136, 163, or 182 toward Liniers). Highly recommended with kids: on Saturdays the children's train built in 1908 operates (10am–6pm).

35__El Ateneo Bookstore

Browsing in the golden movie palace

The stalls and upper circles of a theater dating from 1903 are occupied by rows of books today. In the boxes at the front stand couches where you can sit to browse, and the stage has been turned into a café with a piano that provides suitable background music. Above all of this is spread a romantic painting by an Italian artist symbolizing the end of World War I. A female figure on steps surrounded by flowers is an allegory of peace, and dark clouds drive away the storms of war. This was the theme that an Austrian, Max Glücksmann, wanted to see on the huge dome when, in 1919, he bought the Teatro Nacional, restored it, and named it Grand Splendid.

Glücksmann made the theater into one of the most modern in the city. It was always at the cutting edge, a pioneer of the movies, venue for the first ever screening in Argentina of a film with a soundtrack. From here the country's very first radio broadcasts were transmitted, too. There followed several years when it alternated between being a theater and a cinema, but after 1973 it was solely devoted to screening films.

In February 2000, the El Ateneo chain rented the theater and converted it into the largest bookstore in South America. The character and many of the details of this magnificent auditorium have been retained. Behind the curtain is an old fuse box that is worth taking note of. The lettering above the entrance, the golden balustrades, the ornamentation, and the velvet curtain – all of this remains in its original state, making El Ateneo Grand Splendid an imposing literary experience.

Buenos Aires, by the way, has the world's highest density of bookstores, with 25 of them per 100,000 inhabitants. And with El Ateneo it now has one of the most beautiful. The only one that could compete with it is Selexyz Dominicanen in Maastricht, which is accommodated in an 800-year-old church.

Address Av. Santa Fe 1860, Recoleta, CABA | **Getting there** Subte D to Callao; bus 10, 12, 37, 39, 101, 108, 124, 132, 150, or 152 | **Hours** Mon–Thu 9am–10pm, Fri & Sat 9am–midnight, Sun noon–10pm | **Tip** Eight *cuadras* up Santa Fe (2729, Subte Station Pueyrredón), the attractive Patio del Liceo is home to small shops and exhibition spaces for urban art and design. On the first floor, in the bar Silla Eléctrica, stand-up comedy in Spanish is performed almost every evening (dates on Facebook).

36 El Chonino

Homage to the Argentinian Inspector Rex

What other dog will ever succeed as well as Chonino in gaining recognition in its own country?

From television, we are acquainted with Lassie, and Austrian TV once screened a series about the police dog Inspector Rex. Chonino, however, is no canine film actor but a real-life hero. A German shepherd dog, he was eight years old and had five years' professional experience when, on the rainy night of June 2, 1983 he went out on the beat in Villa Devoto with his handler Luis Sibert and Sibert's colleague Eduardo Ianni. When the officers stopped two suspicious men and demanded to see their identity, things turned violent, and shots rang out. Chonino intervened at just the right moment and leaped heroically to protect his handler when the criminals fired again. The bullet that was meant for Sibert pierced Chonino's heart and killed him. Sibert survived, but his colleague Ianni died too.

When the dog was later examined, part of the coat pocket of one of the suspects, including his ID card, was found in Chonino's mouth. A few days later the criminals, who had been wanted men for some time, were discovered and arrested. Chonino had not only saved his handler's life, and sacrificed his own while doing so, but had secured the decisive piece of evidence only moments before his death.

Today, this courageous German shepherd dog has received the honour that he deserves: a statue of him, cast in bronze, stands on the premises of the federal police, a street in Palermo bears his name, and the anniversary of his death has been commemorated for almost 20 years now as "day of the dog." If you would like to investigate the story more closely, you can take a close-up look of the dead hero: his skeleton is on display in the municipal police museum. The bullet hole in his shoulder blade is marked with a red circle. It was fired at him from a nine-millimeter pistol.

Address Museo de la Policía, San Martín 353, 7th floor (sign in at the gate), San Nicolás, CABA | Getting there Subte B to Florida; bus 6, 22, 24, 26, 28, 29, 33, 50, 56, 61, and others | Hours Mon–Fri 2–6pm | Tip The whole police museum is a well-kept secret, often visited only by police trainees. Alongside items from all eras of policing, an entire room is devoted to the ingenuity of criminals.

37_El Molino Surf Club

Surfin' Buenos Aires!

If you stand on the banks of the Río de la Plata, without a view of Uruguay on the other side, you could imagine that Buenos Aires is on the coast.

This, at least, was what the Spanish thought in 1516 when they surmised that there might be a passage to the Pacific Ocean here. However, as the name reveals, the Río de la Plata is actually a river, and its impressive width can be deceptive. When it flows into the Atlantic, it is no fewer than 219 kilometers across. Although the whole of Buenos Aires lies on the river, you can easily spend several months in the city without ever getting to see the water.

A visit to the El Molino surf club in San Isidro in the north of the Buenos Aires metropolitan area can put this right. Here you see the Río de la Plata from a surprisingly different angle. After some sunbathing on the large area of grass, you will find that the calm waters provide ideal conditions for windsurfing or kitesurfing. Afterwards you can watch the professionals from the roof terrace of the restaurant with its view of the river, and party into the small hours with cocktails or beer. The yellow, green, and red Rasta colors on the walls, the colorful surfboards beneath the ceiling and the reggae DJ create a real Caribbean holiday mood in contrast to the bustle of the big city. The only thing to detract from this is that the water is not turquoise but muddy brown. There are a few sections of the shore near the city center that are truly contaminated, but the river gets its dull color from the high mud content on its bed. This is especially noticeable on satellite images.

Insiders come to El Molino by kayak. For everyone else, the Tren de la Costa is a good alternative. Setting out from the station on Avenida Maipú, you enjoy a wonderful view of the river during the journey and can reconnoitre some excellent spots by the river bank for your next picnic.

Address El Cano 888, Acassuso, San Isidro, Provincia | **Getting there** Mitre train line from Retiro toward Mitre to Bartolomé Mitre, then change to the Tren de la Costa, to Barrancas; bus 168 toward San Isidro | **Hours** Tue–Sun 10am–6pm, longer at some times of year | **Tip** On weekends the Feria del Anticuario antiques market is held at the Barrancas transport stop only a few meters away (see ch. 5).

38 Ex CCDTyE Olimpo

Right among us

"Ex CCDTyE Olimpo" stands for Ex Centro Clandestino de Detención, Tortura y Exterminio Olimpo. The name says everything about what happened here between August 1978 and January 1979: about 650 people died in this secret prison, place of torture, and death camp. Olimpo was part of a network of detention centers during the last military dictatorship. The main such center was ESMA, the technical school of the navy (see ch. 24), where a memorial site established in 2004 has received much attention. Ex Olimpo, in contrast, has been far less widely noticed nationally and internationally.

Even more obviously than ESMA, Olimpo was situated in the middle of a residential area in the district of Veléz Sarsfield. When the military confiscated this former tram depot, they officially set up a motor repair store there. In reality they converted it to a place of torture. At the entrance, they attached a sign bearing the following words: "A Warm Welcome to the Olympus of the Gods." In 1978 the first prisoners were brought here blindfold.

After the restoration of democracy, the premises were at first in the hands of the federal police. In 1999, the film *Garage Olimpo* prompted the first public discussions about what had happened here, and in 2004 the site was finally handed over to a commission made up of survivors, neighbors, and human rights groups. A lot has happened since then. Surveys were held to find out what people from the *barrio* know about the history of Olimpo. The office building, the place where the atrocities took place, was carefully preserved, and in 2015 the rest of the site was made into a park and event venue by cooperatives from the surrounding area. The aim is to establish here the opposite of what the military rulers achieved: cohesion, creativity, and culture. At Ex Olimpo you can see how a city quarter is facing its past.

Address Ramón L. Falcón 4250, Vélez Sársfield, CABA | **Getting there** Sarmiento train line from Once to Floresta; bus 1, 2, 5, 8, 36, 49, 63, 85, 88, 92, and others | **Hours** Memorial site: Mon–Fri 10am–5pm. Events and the latest information: +11/46746471, www.exccdolimpo.org.ar | **Tip** Nearby, there was another, smaller place of torture: Ex CCDTyE Automotores Orletti. If you want to get an impression of the network of prisons, you should also visit this one (Venancio Flores 3519/21, Floresta; Mon–Fri 10am–4pm).

39 Faculty of Humanities

Trotzky, Lenin, and Marx at UBA

If you would like to live (or relive?) the exciting days of the student revolts of 1968, spend a semester studying at the Faculty of Humanities at the University of Buenos Aires (UBA). Even a walk through the building in the Caballito quarter or lunch in one of the student cafés of this area will give you stirring insights into the atmosphere of what must be the most politicized university faculty in Argentina.

The Facultad de Filosofía y Letras is housed in a former tobacco factory. This history sets the scene: smoking is permitted, even in the main halls, and consumption of marijuana is tolerated in the courtyard. The corridors and lecture theaters are chaotically pasted over with hundreds of posters and the banners of various political groups. There are so many student movements and parties that you would need a whole course of study to find your way around the nuances of their political views. For public lectures, *clases públicas*, chairs are often taken out of the lecture hall and placed in the courtyard or even on the street. After all, education is supposed to be accessible to everyone! 'Normal' teaching is frequently interrupted, however, by protests and sit-ins in the lecture theaters – in some semesters there are more cancelations than classes. To lend weight to their demands, for example for a canteen, the students have more than once lit a fire in the courtyard. When the sit-ins drag on for several weeks, lecturers sometimes hold courses in their homes.

Despite (or perhaps because of?) these revolutionary conditions, the standard of teaching at the faculty is very high. The workload of the students is much more onerous than that on most humanities courses at European universities. Depending on the discipline, they are expected to read up to five books per week – always assuming that their seminars actually take place.

Address Puán 480, Caballito, CABA | **Getting there** Subte A to Puán; bus 1, 2, 5, 8, 25, 26, 36, 44, 49, 53, and others | **Hours** Mon–Sat 7am–11pm | **Tip** The small restaurant El Complice (Puán 380) is popular with students.

40_Farmacia de la Estrella

The city's oldest pharmacy

You don't need to have a cold to come to this pharmacy – although one of its old remedies would surely help. The Farmacia de la Estrella, or Star Pharmacy, is the oldest in Buenos Aires. President Rivadavia, concerned about the welfare of the *porteños*, arranged its foundation in 1834. Rivadavia recruited the Italian botanist and biochemist Dr. Pablo Ferrari, who was the first pharmacist to work here. Independence had been gained from Spain little more than 20 years previously, but Argentina was not able or willing to do without European know-how. It was typical of those times that the pharmacy was placed opposite a church, so that in case of emergency a patient could find the way by heading for the tower.

Today, the Farmacia de la Estrella is truly a living exhibition, as it is still in operation yet at the same time is part of the municipal museum in the same building. As soon as you enter, you find yourself standing on a mosaic of Venetian tiles, and the inventory quickly attracts your attention: antique walnut furnishings, Carrara marble, and Italian glass decorate the large room. The ceiling is covered with paintings by the Italian artist Carlos Barberis, illustrating the triumph of medicine over disease. It is rumored that the daughter-in-law of the second owner, Don Silvestre Demarchi, was the model for one of the goddesses shown here. When he died, his sons took over the business and expanded it into one of the leading medical wholesalers in South America.

The Farmacia de la Estrella is still a highly regarded institution. The current pharmacist has been serving his customers for more than 25 years. Alongside modern medicines and colorful drugstore items, the ancient shelves still contain mixtures made according to the original recipes, probably as Rivadavia prepared them: manetti syrup for digestive problems, and a stomach tonic called Hesperidin.

Address Defensa 201, Montserrat, CABA | Getting there Subte A to Plaza de Mayo, Subte D to Catedral, Subte E to Bolívar; bus 2, 8, 22, 24, 28, 29, 56, 64, 86, 91, and others | Hours Mon–Fri 8am–8pm, Sat 8am–1pm | Tip A few minutes' walk away at Av. de Mayo 825 is one of the city's oldest cafés, the famous Café Tortoni (Mon–Fri from 8am, dates of events such as tango shown on the website).

41_The Feria de Mataderos

Folklore, crafts, and culinary treats

Ferias – craft markets with food stalls and street music – are dime a dozen in this city. The best-known *ferias* are held on Plaza Dorrego in San Telmo, on Plaza Francia in Recoleta, and on Plaza Serrano in Palermo. To reach the Feria de Mataderos you have to travel out to the furthest edge of the city. This district was long seen as a hub between the Capital and the Provincia.

It was therefore probably no coincidence that a *feria* sprang up on the marketplace in Mataderos in the mid-1980s. Argentina had just returned to democratic government, and people were beginning to take possession of public spaces again. Furthermore, the question of identity was in the minds of many Argentinians at this time. For *provincianos* in Buenos Aires, the *feria* is a place where they can express their identity. Folk dances such as the chacarera and zamba are performed here – on the stage or below it on the sidewalk. From Tierra del Fuego or Jujuy, in jeans or folk costume, young or old: here people bask in memories of their own lives or those of their grandparents in the provinces.

There are 300 stands that display the products of various artists and craftspeople spread out beneath the walls of the Mercado de Liniers, which opened in 1901. It was once the city's principal slaughterhouse and gave its name to the district – Mataderos means "cattleyard and abattoir."

Although this activity moved out in the 1980s, 9,000 cattle are still auctioned here every day. So it is not surprising that a faint whiff of the cattle corral mingles with the fine aromas of freshly grilled beef and toffee apples on the *feria*. The range of goods on sale extends from earthenware and leather items to jewelry and woven fabrics. Here you are guaranteed to find truly authentic souvenirs at fair prices. A statue of the gaucho Resero, the symbol of Mataderos, looks down on the bustle of the market.

Address Av. de los Corrales 6500, Mataderos, CABA | **Getting there** Subte E (Plaza de los Virreyes), then bus 97, 103, or 141. If you don't know your way around, take a taxi from the Subte station. | **Hours** Sun from 11am, in Feb also Sat from 6pm | **Tip** On the corner in front of the stage (de La Torre 2407) is a traditional bar, El Oviedo, which opened in 1900 and was frequented by workers from the abbattoir.

42 The Fileteado Workshop

A lost art form resurrected

Fileteado is a kind of ornamental painting typical of Buenos Aires. Precise lines, trailing plants, three-dimensional effects and a conscious overloading of the image are the foundations of this craft. At the center there is usually a humorous saying or a tango symbol framed by flags in the Argentinian national colors, garlands of leaves, cornucopias, and flowers.

Fileteado was born in Buenos Aires at the beginning of the 20th century as simple decoration on trucks, and almost all buses used to be completely covered in *fileteados*. In 1975 the city authorities decided this had got out of hand and prohibited the paintings, as the numbers of the buses and their destinations had become hard to identify. Considered an inferior art form, *fileteado* disappeared from view until the tourist boom at the start of the new millennium rediscovered it. Today, its colorful patterns adorn store windows, restaurant signs, posters, and furniture, especially in the San Telmo, Almagro, and Boedo districts.

Miguel Angel is one of the few people who have learned the art of *fileteado* from scratch. His small workshop in San Telmo has no website, but his talents have become known by word of mouth: "I have painted almost all the stores in this street," he says proudly. Since December 2, 2015, the day he learned from the newspaper that *fileteado porteño* had been declared Intangible World Heritage by UNESCO, his telephone has never stopped ringing. More and more people want to take a course with the *fileteador* Angel. Once forbidden, this art form is in fashion again.

Even if you have no commission for him, Miguel is pleased to show how his works are created. For "filleting" he needs brushes with six-centimeter-long hairs, and above all a steady hand. When you next enter a restaurant in Buenos Aires, look closely at the sign above the door: it has definitely not been printed.

Address Chile 886, San Telmo, CABA | **Getting there** Subte C and E to Independencia; bus 2, 9, 10, 17, 45, 59, 67, 70, 91, 98, 100, 103, 129M, or 195 | **Hours** Mon–Fri 9am–7pm, closed for lunch hour; information on tours with the fileteado workshop from Miguel at tours@054online.com and +11/23187685 | **Tip** Three *cuadras* further is a nice café where you can get a good evening meal. Sometimes there is live piano music: Café La Poesía (Chile 502, daily 8–2am).

43 Floralis Genérica

The queen of flowers, made of aluminum

In 2002, the architect Eduardo Catalano wanted to give his home town a new landmark, so he designed this flower, made from aluminum. On postcards the obelisk may be dominant, but the Floralis Genérica has become something like the unofficial emblem of Buenos Aires.

What is special about the flower is that it moves. Every morning at eight o' clock it opens in its turquoise-colored pool, spreads its six petals and shows its stamens. In the evening, it closes them again – except on the first day of spring, the national holiday on May 25, Christmas Eve and New Year's Eve: on these occasions, it also flowers at night.

On every other day, the interior of Floralis Genérica glows in futuristic red and purple. Steven Spielberg's E.T. would surely have climbed inside it to phone home. If the wind blows at a speed of more than 80 kilometers per hour, the huge flower, which weighs 18 tonnes and is 23 meters high, sensibly closes automatically, even in daytime.

Despite these precautions, a few years after the opening, a storm destroyed the hydraulic mechanism. All attempts to repair it failed, as the company that had once constructed the sculpture had disappeared from the country, taking the plans with it. And the designer was no longer able to help with information, as he had died. It was not until June 2015 that Floralis Genérica could flower again, following six months of work by several companies and the Technical University to take it to pieces and repair the mechanism.

Now, once again, the flower is the queen of the Plaza de las Naciones Unidas. When the sun shines, children playing and couples enjoying a drink of mate on the lawns are reflected in Floralis Genérica – and so are the skyscrapers of Recoleta. Hardly anyone knows the proper name of this work of art. It is simply too long. It is therefore generally known simply as *La Flor* – the flower.

Address Plaza de las Naciones Unidas, Av. Figueroa Alcorta and Austria, Recoleta, CABA | **Getting there** Bus 17, 61, 62, 67, 92, 93, 110, 124, or 130 | **Tip** To the east of the park is the imposing building of the law faculty (Av. Figueroa Alcorta 2263). If it is open, don't fail to take a look inside the lobby, which has the nickname "salon of lost steps."

44 Galería Bond Street

Punk, tattoos, and avant-garde

Bond Street in London is home to the most elegant boutiques, the most expensive jewelers, and the least affordable antiques. The same description no longer fits the gallery of the same name in Buenos Aires. Built in 1963, when it was the most modern shopping arcade in the city, it set its sights on high society, just like its namesake in London. Today, it is the diametric opposite of the famous Bond Street in the United Kingdom.

As a consequence of the economic disaster of dictatorship, in the 1980s the expensive boutiques disappeared from the galería. In their place, artists and outfitters from all kinds of different subcultures moved in. First to arrive were punk clothing and heavy-metal CDs, followed by alternative designers, and skateboard stores. In the 1990s they were joined by the tattoo parlors. Nowhere in Argentina, and quite possibly nowhere in the whole of South America, is there such a concentration of tattoo stores in one place as at Bond Street. Diego Maradona and the cult German punk band Die Toten Hosen came here to style themselves.

As a new customer group arrived, the appearance of the galería changed. Graffiti were sprayed all over the escalators, the bronze balustrades were covered with stickers, and metal sculptures by local underground avant-garde artists were to be seen. In this way Bond Street became not only the shopping mall of preference for alternative scenes, but also an unconventional space for art at the heart of Recoleta, the quarter of the rich.

To put it in a nutshell: Bond Street is the place to which traders gravitate who do not match the normal commercial life of the city, and the place where kids kit themselves out with fashionable and musical accessories for their brands of social criticism. A lot of fashion punks mix here with the genuine revolutionaries, and Bond Street is somewhere between Hello Kitty and heavy metal.

Address Av. Santa Fe 1670, Recoleta, CABA | Getting there Subte D to Callao; bus 12, 29, 37, 39, 60, 106, 109, 111, 140, 142, 150, 151, or 152 | Hours Mon–Sat 11am–8pm | Tip Three *cuadras* to the east lies 5ta Avenida, another unusual galería, mainly for vintage and second-hand stores (Av. Santa Fe 1270, Mon–Sat 8am–8pm).

45 Galpón Orgánico

Solidarity – an alternative to supermarkets

At the end of a paved road, along the tracks of Lacroze station, stands "the shed," surrounded by rusting, abandoned rail trucks. El Galpón is a farmers' market that works on the principles of cooperation and solidarity. Twice a week, producers from Buenos Aires Provincia come here to sell organic, regional wares at 18 stalls: wine, cheese, sausage, honey, fruit juice, and vegan chocolate – but also cosmetics, water filters, and recycled paper bags from a therapy institution. In Galpón you can find absolutely everything that makes life healthier, protects the environment, and lends a basis of solidarity to the economy.

A small restaurant prepares meals using products sold on the market. If you don't know what to do with quinoa or amaranth in your kitchen, you will find inspiration here. On Saturdays, there is a barbecue – with organic meat on the grill, as well as vegetables, of course. Organic, vegetarian, and vegan diets are now fashionable even in Argentina, the meat-eating nation par excellence. Ten years ago, when the Asociación Mutual Sentimiento established the market, the situation was different. The Asociación has its roots in the solidarity economy and is keen to emphasise that El Galpón is not a supermarket, where consumption is anonymous. It wants to promote a dialog between city dwellers and producers that makes the methods and conditions of production apparent and sets fair prices. "Taking the mask off eating," is how Federico, the market coordinator, describes this.

It is therefore not surprising that this old railway shed was among the sites for exchange transactions in the solidarity economy during the crisis of 2001. When people could no longer get cash from the bank, they were dependent on bartering. Today, this is no longer necessary, but mutual benefit and cooperation remains the concept of trading in the railway shed.

Address Av. Federico Lacroze 4171 (200 meters along the paved road), Chacarita, CABA | **Getting there** Urquiza train line to Lacroze, Subte B to Lacroze; bus 42, 44, 47, 63, 65, 71, 111, 123, or 127 | **Hours** Wed & Sat 9am–6pm | **Tip** You can't miss the huge Chacarita Cemetery (see ch. 26) opposite Lacroze station, and don't fail to visit it!

46 The Gautier Telescope

An abandoned gem dating from 1882

Beneath the dome of the observatory of the Asociación Argentina Amigos de la Astronomía (AAAA) is a gem for star-gazers. This telescope by the French maker Gautier was constructed in 1882. A delegation from the venerable Paris observatory wanted to observe the transit of Venus from Argentina. This extremely rare phenomenon, in which Venus passes in front of the sun, only takes place four times every 243 years. On December 6, 1882, it was expected to be visible with great clarity from the southern hemisphere. After months of preparation, the big day ended in disappointment: with a cloudy sky. The delegation had to return to France without making any new discoveries, and left its equipment behind in Argentina. In France they would not have been able to make use of it, as the telescope is not adjustable, and can focus on the planets only when it is set up in Argentinian latitudes. For astronomy in Argentina, however, this was a stroke of luck, and it initiated the founding of an observatory for the National University of La Plata.

When this national training center for astronomers was modernized in 1944 it presented the old Gautier telescope to the AAAA in Buenos Aires. The association had just opened its own observatory in the Parque Centenario. Since then, the telescope with its 220-millimeter shutter and focal length of 3,300 millimeters has been the centerpiece of the station. Only the wooden barrel had to be replaced, as it had become warped. Everything else – the mount, the optics, and the clockwork mechanism – is original and still in perfect working order. When guided tours are held, visitors can look at the stars through it. And thanks to a second telescope, made by the company Carl Zeiss in 1912, astronomy enthusiasts have a second gem.

If you should happen to be in Buenos Aires on December 11, 2117, you can observe the next transit of Venus.

Address Parque Centenario, Av. Patricias Argentinas 550, Caballito, CABA | **Getting there** Subte B to Ángel Gallardo; bus 15, 24, 36, 42, 55, 57, 65, 71, 76, 92, and others | **Hours** Mon–Sat 7–11pm. Tours with a view through the telescope every Fri & Sat after dusk (except on cloudy days). Call for exact times: +11/48633366 or www.amigosdelaastronomia.org. Special events are held for unusual astronomical phenomena. | **Tip** In the Parque Centenario there are dinosaur skeletons from Patagonia in the Natural History Museum and rare meteorites.

47 Guido's Bar

Where you eat what you are given

This Italian restaurant is run according to a simple and brilliant concept: there is no menu. The only choice you are given is: "tinto o blanco" – red wine or white? The waiters decide what you are served. Does this sound impertinent? When the owner, Carlos Soto, explains his philosophy, you wonder why everyone does not work this way. In a restaurant you want to eat well in company. But in reality, hungry guests first of all get white bread and mayonnaise. At this the conversation stops, because everyone is eating bread and staring at the menu. As they do so, most people look not only at the dishes on offer but also at the prices.

Guido's Bar is different: you have hardly sat down before excellent antipasti are placed on the table. Less than a minute later your glasses have been filled, and the conversation moves on. You are given a selection, one by one, of delicious dishes – risotto, pasta, and pizza, including a lot of vegetarian options. If you look across to the next table, you will see a completely different menu. Drinks, dessert, and espresso are included. The idea works, not least because the food is exceptionally good.

Carlos learned to cook in Italy as a young man, and has been running this restaurant next to the zoo in Palermo for 35 years. When he started, it was a dive. The wild mix of decoration, consisting of posters of Italy, football shirts, and Kama Sutra calendars is a vivid reminder of those days.

Then the district changed. More and more expensive high-rises were built. The restaurant is the last single-story building in the *barrio*. As a new, upmarket clientele came, Carlos raised his prices. If you come here by chance, relying on the internet description that promises a "snack bar," you will probably get a shock when you see the bill. But for those who know what to expect, Guido's Bar simply has cult status.

Address República de la India 2843, Palermo, CABA | **Getting there** Subte D to Plaza Italia; bus 10, 37, 41, 59, 60, 64, 93, 95, 108, 110, 118, 128, 160, 188 | **Hours** Mon–Sat 8am–midnight or later | **Tip** Three *cuadras* away, the Japanese Garden (Av. Casares 2966, daily 10am–6pm) is worth seeing, and it has a restaurant (daily 10am–6pm & 7:30pm–midnight, except Tue evening).

48_The Historic Tram

Next stop Caballito

The age of the tram in Buenos Aires has left many traces in the city. Everywhere, between cobblestones and asphalt, the rails of the once-so-vital *tranvía* appear. This is the case in Caballito, where life is breathed back into the old days every weekend. On the "tramway histórico" you can take a two-kilometer trip and indulge in nostalgia. Since 1980 an association called Amigos del Tranvía (Friends of the Tramway) has looked after a collection of historic tramcars from various decades.

For a hundred years, the tram was the most important means of transport in Bueno Aires. The first one, in 1863, was pulled by horses, linking the Retiro station with Plaza de Mayo. From 1897 the horses were replaced by steam power, then by electricity. At the peak of the tram network in the mid-1920s, 99 lines and 3,000 trams moved on 875 kilometers of track. In 1913, Line A, the first underground railway in the southern hemisphere, was added. The original carriages with their wooden seats were in service until 2013. The last overground tram was taken out of service in 1963. Privatization arrived, and trams had to make way for cheaper buses made in Germany, England, and Brazil.

Thanks to the Amigos del Tranvía, not all of the old trams disappeared. The association saved several of these old treasures and made them operational again in the new age of travel. The oldest model dates from 1927. An essential part of the leisure outings on weekends are a driver and conductor, dressed in the appropriate uniform. And before the tram trundles off, all the passengers are given an authentic ticket printed in the style of the old days.

As a feeder service for the Subte E line, since 1987 a tram made in Argentina, the Pre-Metro, has once again been rumbling through the *barrios* at the margins of the city. But it has no hope of competing with the glory of the Tramway Histórico.

Address Corner of Emilio Mitre and José Bonifacio, Caballito, CABA stop on the corner opposite the depot | **Getting there** Sarmiento train from Once to Caballito, then walk 600 meters, or Subte A to Primera Junta, Subte E to Emilio Mitre; bus 1, 2, 5, 8, 25, 26, 36, 49, 53, 55, and others | **Hours** Free trips on Sat, Sun, & holidays, Mar–Nov 4–7:30pm, Dec–Feb 5–8:30pm, all year round Sun 10am–1:30pm every 25 minutes | **Tip** Finish your trip back in time by drinking coffee at the hairdresser-café La Época (see ch. 11) 600 meters away.

49 The Holocaust Memorial

The first one in a Christian church

When the glass case was inaugurated in Buenos Aires Cathedral in 1997, it was the world's first Holocaust memorial inside a Christian church. It hangs in the chapel of the Virgin of Luján in the nave of the Catedral Metropolitana on Plaza de Mayo at the center of the city. Behind glass are fragments of Hebrew prayer and song books that come from European concentration camps and ghettos. The case also contains documents from the buildings of the Israeli embassy and the Jewish arts center AMIA (see ch. 98) in Buenos Aires, which were destroyed in the 1990s by bombings that caused fatalities. Jewish symbols such as the Star of David and the menorah have been engraved into the frame.

The Argentinian Jewish activist Baruch Tenembaum had the idea of creating this memorial. Now over 80 years old, for decades he has been campaigning for dialog between religions. In 1995, he arranged a meeting between Pope John Paul II and Emilie Schindler, the widow of the famous Oskar Schindler who saved the lives of hundreds of Jews. After World War II she emigrated to South America with her husband. Until shortly before her death in 2001, Emilie lived in Buenos Aires and met Tenembaum there. In 2009, Tenembaum was even nominated for the Nobel Prize for Peace, which in the end went to Barack Obama.

The existence of a Shoah monument in the most important Catholic church in the country had a significant effect on the relations between Argentinian Christians and Jews. In 2014, a memorial service was held here for Cardinal Quarracino, who had consecrated the monument before his death in 1998. During the ceremony, a rabbi said the Jewish Kaddish prayer for the cardinal in Hebrew. This, too, was unprecedented at the time. In the same year, the Lutheran Church of Our Father in Berlin installed a replica of the memorial in the presence of Tenembaum.

Address Av. Rivadavia and San Martín, San Nicolás, CABA | **Getting there** Subte A to Plaza de Mayo, Subte D to Catedral, Subte E to Bolívar; bus 2, 8, 20, 22, 24, 28, 29, 56, 64, 86, and others | **Hours** Mon–Thu 9am–7pm, Fri 9am–5pm, Sun 1–6:30pm | **Tip** Diagonally opposite stands the Cabildo, the official seat of government of the Spanish viceroys. Today it houses a museum about the May Revolution.

50 Hotel B.A.U.E.N.

Support a social cause in your sleep

At the height of the military dictatorship in 1978, and in connection with the football World Cup in Argentina, the BAUEN hotel was built. The state lent $5 million to the businessman Marcelo Iurcovich for construction of this 20-story building with 222 rooms. He never repaid the loan, but evaded taxes and made millions in profit. In the 1990s, as more and more international hotel chains came to the country, BAUEN floundered. In 1997, Iurcovich sold it to a Chilean company, but on December 28, 2001 the hotel finally went bankrupt and the remaining 80 employees were out of work – in the middle of Argentina's worst economic crisis. Unemployment reached a record level.

On March 20, 2003 former staff members, supported by the National Movement for Taking Back Companies, which had emerged after the economic crisis, occupied the empty building. They put it in order again and founded a cooperative that could carry on business legally. They only had to make a small change to the name. Now B.A.U.E.N. is written with a dot after each letter, and stands for Cooperativa Buenos Aires Una Empresa Nacional. They succeeded in doing what nobody thought possible: the hotel was profitable, and created 150 jobs. Since then, there have been no hierarchies in the hotel. The only controls are the employees' conscience and the democratic decisions of the cooperative.

In late 2014, not for the first time, the hotel employees were threatened with eviction. The former owner had bought it back from the Chilean company, and now laid claim to the building. So far it has been possible to prevent all attempts at eviction, and guests can therefore support the workers' struggle in their sleep. But beware: B.A.U.E.N. should not be confused with the BAUEN Suite round the corner. The latter is the only part of the company that remains in the hands of Iurcovich.

Address Av. Callao 360, San Nicolás, CABA, www.bauenhotel.com.ar | **Getting there** Subte B to Callao; bus 5, 6, 7, 12, 24, 26, 37, 50, 60, 115, 124, 146, 150, or 180 | **Hours** Reception open round the clock, the café-restaurant in chic 1970s style daily 7am–midnight | **Tip** Just round the corner, between Av. Corrientes and Lavalle, is a strange little S-shaped street, Enrique Santos Discepolo, along which a train once ran. A plaque on the building at the corner of Lavalle commemorates its maiden journey in 1858.

51 Hotel de Inmigrantes

Where new arrivals stayed

Thousands of people who arrived at the port of Buenos Aires in the 20th century stayed at the Hotel de Inmigrantes. "Hotel" is not exactly the right word for it. It was in fact mass accommodation with big dormitories and shared bathrooms. Today, this impressive building, which dates from 1906, is a museum telling the story of people who came to South America in search of a new life. This makes it the counterpart of the emigration museums in European ports such as BallinStadt in Hamburg.

The foundation of a charity for immigration made it possible to build the Hotel de Inmigrantes, the last and largest of four such institutions that catered for a constantly growing number of immigrants. One hundred meters long and four stories high, the building had four residential sections on each floor and could provide shelter for 4,000 people altogether. After their arrival, the immigrants were channeled systematically through the building: from the registration point and the labor office to the medical ward and then through to the accommodation. Many of them were housed free of charge until they had found work and a place to live.

The Hotel de Inmigrantes remained in operation until 1953. In the 1990s it was declared a national historic monument. Today, it houses the National Museum of Immigration, and a center for contemporary art has been attached. As well as a historical archive, which keeps documents including the old passenger lists, the lively and modern exhibition illustrates everyday life in the hotel. Visitors see the spartan bunks and immigrants' personal possessions such as passports, photos, and suitcases. The stairwells and corridors with their high ceilings and white-tiled walls and floors have been retained in their original condition. The themes of the temporary art exhibitions are global issues such as economic and forced migration.

Address Av. Antártida Argentina 1355, Retiro, CABA | Getting there San Martín, Mitre and Belgrano Norte train lines, or Subte C to Retiro; bus 5, 6, 7, 9, 20, 22, 23, 28, 33, 50, and others | Hours Tue–Sun noon–8pm, tours in Spanish, brochure also in English | Tip Nearby on Plaza Canadá, toward the stations, is a totem made by Native Canadians.

52 The Jesuit Tunnels

A historic feat of engineering by monks

These short sections of tunnel on Manzana de las Luces give a hint of what lies behind the sea of houses in the city center: an ingenious network of subterranean passages that connected the most important places in colonial Buenos Aires. The network was built in the 17th century by the Jesuits, who are generally known to have been skilled engineers. In 1608, this religious order came to Buenos Aires, building the city's first church and a school between the streets that are now called Perú and Bolívar. The outstanding educational role played by the Jesuits' site gave it the name Manzana de las Luces: the block of enlightenment.

The existence of the mysterious tunnels was known, as they were marked on a map dating from 1780, but they were not rediscovered until 1912, when the ground started collapsing during construction work and revealed a network of vaults beneath. The tunnels are about six meters below the ground. They are two meters high and ninety centimeters wide on average. They served as routes for communication and defense, but were also used by smugglers in the period when trade was controlled by Spain.

In the building boom of the 12th century, most of them were filled in, torn down, or built upon. The only way to admire a part of the system is to take a guided tour of Manzana de las Luces. Historians believe that there are least four passageways, one of which leads as far as the Cabildo on Plaza de Mayo. The Casa Rosada (see ch. 10) is also said to have tunnels beneath it. There is a further entrance in the Jesuit school building. In 2013, pupils of the school broke open the padlock and passed through the tunnels to the Church of San Ignacio, a deed that attracted more publicity for the underground system. Nobody knows exactly how extensive the network is. The myths that surround it are probably greater than the reality.

Address Perú 272, Monserrat, CABA | **Getting there** Subte A to Perú, Subte D to Catedral, Subte E to Bolívar; bus 2, 8, 22, 24, 28, 29, 56, 64, 86, 91, and others | **Hours** Tours Mon–Fri 3pm, Sat & Sun 3pm, 4:30pm, & 6pm | **Tip** At the northernmost tip of the manzana is La Librería del Avila with its small café. As books have been sold here since 1785, it is thought to be the city's oldest bookstore (Adolfo Alsina 500, Mon–Fri 8:30am–8pm, Sat 10am–3pm).

53 The Juana Azurduy Monument

A political battle about interpreting history

Brave, fearless, heroic – history books all over the world ascribe these qualities to men. Thus the collective memory of South America is dominated by male heroes such as the Argentinian general San Martín and the Venezuelan freedom fighter Simón Bolívar. Their presence as statues in the streets and parks of the continent reinforce this. The monument to the female Bolivian freedom fighter Juana Azurduy de Padilla is therefore, regrettably, out of the ordinary.

The sight of this nine-meter-high female figure makes a strong impression. Standing on a pyramid of the Andean Tiahuanaco culture, Azurduy holds a sword in her left hand while raising her right hand to protect the people and the child on her back. The sculptor succeeded in lending overwhelming vital energy to this bulky statue with a weight of 25 tonnes. The Bolivian president Evo Morales paid for the heroic monument, which cost $1 million, and inaugurated it together with President Cristina Kirchner in 2015.

What makes this controversial is that Azurduy was set up behind the presidential palace, exactly on the spot where a statue of Christopher Columbus once stood. The latter was put in store and re-erected in 2017 on the Costanera. For the Kirchner government, this had a doubly symbolic meaning. First, a freedom fighter from the indigenous population was honored instead of a conqueror and subjugator of the indigenous peoples. And second, the importance of women in the history of the continent was made publicly visible.

Less than two years after its inauguration, the new neoliberal government under Macri spent a lot of money to move Juana Azurduy – officially because of flaws on the exterior. Now it stands in front of the Centro Cultural Kirchner. Columbus, for his part, remains on the urban margins close to the city airport Aeroparque.

Address In front of the Centro Cultural Kirchner, Sarmiento 151, San Nicolás, CABA | Getting there Subte B to Leandro N. Alem; bus 4, 6, 7, 20, 22, 23, 26, 28, 29, 33, and others | Hours Viewable from the outside only | Tip If you are here, pay a visit to the Centro Cultural Kirchner in what used to be the main post office. Named for the deceased ex-president Nestor Kirchner, it opened in 2015. The huge concert hall, "the blue whale," is most impressive (tours Sat, Sun, holidays 2pm & 3:30pm, booking required; event listings: www.cck.gob.ar).

54 The Kavanagh Building

Revenge is tall

Corina Kavanagh was furious, absolutely furious! She had fallen in love with the son of the aristocrat Mercedes Castellanos de Anchorena, better known as Condesa Pontificia María Luisa de las Mercedes Castellanos de la Iglesia. However, the noble lady had made sure that her son broke off the relationship with Corina. A marriage to a nouveau riche middle-class woman was beneath the dignity of her "old money" aristocratic family. Corina Kavanagh's answer to this slight was to take her whole inheritance and build a huge edifice on the east side of Plaza San Martín. Here it completely concealed the basilica behind, which her enemy had ordered to be constructed as the family tomb. The Anchorenas lived on the other side of the plaza in the Palacio San Martín, and now had no view of their church – the worst punishment she could have chosen.

When the building was completed in 1936 after only 14 months' construction time, it not only gave satisfaction to Corina but also broke several records. At 120 meters and with 33 stories, for a time it was the tallest building in South America, and the first in Argentina with air conditioning and a swimming pool. It won several awards at that time. In 1999, UNESCO declared it part of the World Heritage of modern architecture, and in 2013 the newspaper *Clarín* voted it the most beautiful building in the city. To this day, it has no intercom system. Visitors have to go to the concierge, who informs the residents above by phone of their arrival.

Until her death in 1984 Corina lived on the 14th floor. Her apartment, which occupies the whole of that floor, was sold in 2008 for $5.9 million.

It was to be an act of eternal revenge. Nobody talks about the Anchorena family today, but the Edificio Kavanagh is well known. To reach the basilica you have to walk along a lane. Its name is Corina Kavanagh.

Address Florida 1065, Retiro, CABA | **Getting there** Subte C to San Martín; bus 6, 7, 9, 20, 22, 23, 26, 28, 33, 45, and others | **Hours** Viewable from the outside only | **Tip** Three *cuadras* away is the cosy rustic bar and restaurant Bárbaro (Tres Sargentos 415, Mon–Sat 9–2am).

55 King Fahd Mosque

Open to all

The King Fahd Mosque in Palermo was built in 1996 while Carlos Menem was president. Menem is the child of immigrants from Syria, and because some people seemingly did not know where Syria is, they called him "El Turco," the Turk. To become president, he had to convert to Christianity, but he provided an important impetus for construction of the mosque. He allowed the Islamic community to have a site of 3.5 hectares free of charge. The king of Saudi Arabia paid for the building and still bears its running costs.

With its two minarets, large prayer hall, school, and arts center, this is the largest mosque in Latin America. It can hold up to 1,500 worshippers, but is only full during Ramadan. When it was built, the size of the Muslim population was expected to grow more steeply. Only about one percent of the 43 million Argentinians are adherents of Islam, half of whom live in Buenos Aires.

The architect of the complex with its unadorned style and elements of Arab architecture was a Saudi, and the materials were provided by Argentinian companies. This national identity is important to the Islamic community. Most of its members have Argentinian citizenship. Friendly sports games are often held on the field attached to the mosque complex. The arts center and the state-recognized primary school are used by non-Muslims, who make up 90 percent of the pupils. The Saudi Arabian influence is no secret: the site is diplomatic territory, and among the members of the governing council are both Argentinians and Saudis.

The level of religious tolerance in Buenos Aires is high. No protests whatever accompanied construction of the mosque, and it opens its doors to visitors three times weekly. During the guided tours, all questions about Islamic religion and culture, no matter how naïve, are patiently answered, which is intended to clear away prejudices.

Address Corner of Av. Bullrich 55 and Cerviño, Palermo, CABA | **Getting there** San Martín train from Retiro to Palermo, Mitre train from Retiro to 3 de Febrero, Subte D to Palermo; bus 10, 12, 15, 29, 39, 41, 55, 57, 59, 60, and others | **Hours** Tours Tue, Thu, & Sat at noon, unless it rains. English tours by arrangement for 15 people or more (+11/48991144, info@cciar.com). Wear clothes that cover up well. | **Tip** From the mosque it is only a few paces to the park Bosques de Palermo, where you can take a walk to the Red Riding Hood sculpture (see ch. 85).

56_The Kosher McDonald's

Fast food, approved by the rabbi

Could this be the only travel guide in the world that recommends paying a visit to a McDonald's restaurant?

What could be so special about an outlet of an international fast-food chain, when they are all practically identical across the globe? But this one is different. From outside the difference is only one small, six-letter word, but what's inside the burger is all the more distinctive.

The Abasto shopping center in the Balvanera quarter, better known under the name Once, is home to the only kosher McDonald's restaurant outside Israel. It is even said to have been the first in the world. The fast food served here is prepared strictly according to Jewish kitchen regulations. For those who are not familiar with this: foods whose consumption is permitted by the Torah are known as kosher. Only specified animals may be eaten. Meat and dairy products may not be eaten or prepared together, and no blood may be consumed. And it goes without saying that this restaurant is closed from Friday evening until Saturday evening, i.e. on the Sabbath. Rabbi Daniel Oppenheimer supervises conformity to the rules, as a large, yellow-and-red poster next to the serving counter assures customers.

In this way the famous American hamburger chain has become a clear symbol for the importance and size of the Jewish community in Buenos Aires. Almost 30,000 Orthodox Jews live in the Once district alone.

If you would prefer, for culinary or political reasons, not to dine at McDonald's, you can buy a home-made kosher sausage in one of the numerous Jewish stores in this neighborhood. And if you insist on eating some fast food, don't make the mistake of ordering a cheese-burger. Unless Rabbi Oppenheimer has failed in the performance of his duties, you can be sure that no such item is on the menu in this particular branch of McDonald's.

Address Abasto Shopping, 2nd floor, Av. Corrientes 3247, Balvanera, CABA | **Getting there** Subte B to Carlos Gardel; bus 24, 26, 29, 41, 62, 64, 68, 71, 99, 110, and others | **Hours** Sun–Thu & holidays 10am–11pm; Fri, Sat, & before holidays 10–1am | **Tip** To the west of Abasto Shopping on Pasaje Carlos Gardel you will find a monument to the legendary tango musician and many buildings decorated with *fileteados* (see ch. 42). Round the corner an interesting museum is dedicated to Gardel in his former house (Jean Jaures 735, Mon & Wed–Fri 11am–6pm, tours 1pm & 4pm; Sat, Sun, & holidays 10am–7pm, tours 11am, 3pm, & 5pm).

57 La Cigarra

A no-tell hotel, retro-style

We could have written a book entitled *111 Telos in Buenos Aires That You Should Not Miss*. A *telo* is a hotel that you book by the hour – a typical play on words in Lunfardo, the local slang, in which the syllables of the word "hotel" are reversed. The official name is *albergue transitorio*: transient accommodation. Nowhere in Latin America is there such a high density of these establishments: within the city limits there are about 200 of them, and if you add those in the Buenos Aires Provincia, it would take years to try them all out.

A "no-tell hotel" does not have a sleazy image here. Of course, there are some cheap, ill-ventilated fleapits with bed bugs, but you can also book a luxurious *telo* that is guaranteed to be sensual. For many lovers in a Catholic country they are the only opportunity to spend some intimate time together. On weekends and in the evenings, couples come along; midday customers are having extra-marital affairs. *Telos* are part of the urban culture, across all age groups and social classes.

La Cigarra is one of the oldest in Buenos Aires. In the 1960s it was the setting for two movies. The furnishings and a Marilyn Monroe poster are reminders of those years. Its legally "tolerated activity" operates everywhere as follows: when the intercom buzzes, you enter a dimly lit lobby. A receptionist behind darkened glass discreetly takes your reservation. Depending on the day of the week and time of day, this is valid for a certain number of hours. An illuminated display shows the various categories, for example a room with a mirror on the ceiling or a Jacuzzi. If you pay by credit card or bank card, an invented name appears on the card account. An elevator takes you upstairs. The rooms are fashionably furnished and clean. Towels, toothbrushes, and condoms are provided. Cold drinks can be ordered.

Welcome to the Eldorado of transient accommodation!

Address Godoy Cruz 2883, Palermo, CABA. You can find almost all telos at www.alberguestransitorios.com | **Getting there** Subte D to Palermo; bus 12, 15, 29, 39, 41, 55, 57, 59, 60, 64, and others | **Hours** 24 hours daily: 5-hour periods. Fri, Sat, & before holidays 10pm–6am: 2 hours. Sat, Sun, & holidays 6am–noon: 3 hours; no charge at La Cigarra if it's your birthday | **Tip** The best Arab food in town is within walking distance (10 *cuadras*) at Demashk restaurant (Charcas 3816, Mon–Sat 10am–4pm & 6pm–midnight).

58 Lanchas Almaceneras

Floating supermarkets in the Tigre Delta

About 20 kilometers north of the Argentinian capital, the Tigre Delta forms the boundary of the Buenos Aires metropolitan area. It is an extensive network of canals and rivers with countless islands. Most of them are inhabited. Instead of cars and paved roads there are water taxis, a fire brigade boat, a refuse collection boat, and a floating YPF filling station. All aspects of everyday life are organized on the water.

Every morning a dozen *Lanchas Almaceneras* chug out into the delta. These floating supermarkets are the lifeline of the island dwellers. Every day they provide hundreds of families with food, drinks, charcoal, gas cylinders, and household goods. Some of the boats have been operating here for several generations. According to a fixed schedule, they ply a zigzag course around the waterways, putting in at the private jetties of houses, where the customers are already expecting them. In the Tigre Delta, life is adapted to the environment, not the other way around.

The routes through the system of channels are strictly apportioned among the *lancheros*. There is no competition, and the prices of one hardly differ from the prices of the others. The *Lanchas Almaceneras* are not only a store – they have a vital social role to play in the daily life of the delta. They are an information exchange, a post service, a hub for gossip, and a partner for small talk all rolled into one. If residents realize in the morning that they urgently need something, they phone their lanchero before he leaves port. It might be a fishing hook, condoms, or cigarettes – the emergency orders include all kinds of things.

With luck, you might spot a floating supermarket on a trip to the delta, for example on a tour of Tres Bocas (see ch. 108). Alternatively, go to Puerto de los Frutos on the mainland early in the morning, to see them loading before they set off.

Address Puerto de los Frutos, Las Casuarinas, Tigre, Provincia | **Getting there** The Tren de la Costa stops just after the Delta stop at Puerto de Frutos. The Mitre train to Tigre terminates at the harbor, where passenger boats set off for the delta. | **Tip** Behind Puerto de los Frutos is a big amusement park, the Parque de la Costa, open in summer (Tue–Sun 11am–8pm).

59 Las Heras 2214

Unfinished pseudo-Gothic

Sometimes people make the sign of the cross when they pass this building, believing it is a cathedral. However, there is no point in the gesture here. The structure in Gothic Revival style on Avenida Las Heras in Recoleta was planned for the university Faculty of Law and Social Sciences. The architect, Arturo Prins, had in fact proposed a completely different design, but the heads of the university were gripped by the neo-Gothic fever of the 19th century, which was already out of date by that time. They sent Prins to Europe to find inspiration. His new design, including a lordly-looking tower, 120 meters tall, delighted his clients. And so the foundation stone was laid in 1910 for a faculty building in the neo-Gothic style.

At the outbreak of World War I the costs skyrocketed, and construction was delayed. To make it possible to use at least part of the building for teaching in 1925, the plans were altered. In the end the university decided it would be cheaper to have a new building than to complete this one, and stopped the project in 1938. As the tower was never constructed, today the building looks incomplete, as if the roof had been cut off. This is a pity, as the original drawings, which can be found on the internet, demonstrate. Las Heras 2214 would have been a miniature version of the Victoria Tower of the Palace of Westminster in London, and thus a fitting counterpart to the copy of Big Ben that was given by the United Kingdom to Argentina for the 100th anniversary of its independence and now stands in the Retiro district.

Today, Las Heras 2214 houses the Faculty of Engineering and a museum of science and technology. It is worth looking inside. The monumental steps leading to the lecture halls and the scales that appear in the window glass as a symbol of justice are an obvious reminder of the original intention to make this the Faculty of Law.

Address Av. Las Heras 2214, Recoleta, CABA | **Getting there** Bus 10, 37, 41, 59, 60, 61, 62, 92, 93, 95, 102, 108, 110, or 118 | **Hours** Mon–Fri 9am–7pm, for events on weekends too | **Tip** A few steps away, the terrace of the somewhat overpriced Silver Pub (Vicente López 2176) has the best view of the Recoleta cemetery.

60_The Le Doute Sculpture

A monument to atheism?

Buenos Aires is considered an open-air museum for the visual arts. Almost every park and plaza is embellished with a great national hero or statesman – and all too rarely a stateswoman. But not every work was made to honor a hero. A few of them are devoted to the profound questions of human existence.

On Plaza San Martín in Retiro there stands an example of this. Thousands of people hurry past every day on their way to the station or the bustling shopping street Florida without paying any attention to *Le Doute* ("The Doubt"). A delegation brought this sculpture from Europe in the early 19th century. The delegation had been commissioned by the city government of Buenos Aires to acquire new monuments for public places, as before that time the city had few such works. Some members of the delegation felt sure that *Le Doute* would not find acceptance but, in their enthusiasm for this work by the French artist Louis Henri Cordier, they wanted to give it a try at least.

The sculpture depicts a young Christian believer, sitting thoughtfully over an open Bible while an old man on his right places a hand on his shoulder and seems to be persuading him to call the scriptures into question. It is not easy to express in stone something as abstract as doubt. However, if you look at the expression on the young man's face, you can clearly perceive this doubt.

The doubtful members of the delegation were to be proved wrong: in 1906 the work was installed in public. And who would have thought that, in a religious country like Argentina, it would never give rise to a controversial discussion? Perhaps the alternate interpretation, according to which the two figures represent the Old and the New Testament, was helpful in this respect. Yet if this reading is accepted, it remains unclear why the sculptor incized the words "the doubt" in French on the base of his work.

Address Plaza San Martín near Av. Santa Fe 710, Retiro, CABA | **Getting there** Subte C to General San Martín; bus 7, 9, 45, 70, 106, 108, 132, 150, or 152 | **Tip** A few minutes' walk takes you to the Galerías Pacífico shopping mall (Florida and Av. Córdoba, daily 10am–9pm). If you don't like shopping, you can admire the huge painting on the dome.

61 Little Bolivia

Varieties of potato, Inca Kola, and llama fetuses

A visit to the Bolivian quarter is like taking a trip to La Paz in the Andes. You can watch men eagerly carrying large sacks full of fruit and vegetables through dense crowds of people. With bright yellow Inca Kola and glowing jewelry, these are colorful surroundings. The air is filled with the smell of spices, while the atmosphere is businesslike and simultaneously relaxed.

In the middle of Buenos Aires you can find all the ingredients for Bolivian and Peruvian cuisine, including 20 different kinds of potatoes. You can even stock up on llama fetuses, a traditional sacrificial item, if you are interested. Suárez, a street that branches off Avenida Rivadavia in the eastern district of Liniers, is the main artery of "Little Bolivia."

From the early 20th century onwards, many Bolivians came to their southern neighbor Argentina, initially as migrant workers. Most of them, hoping to find a better life, succeeded in setting up their own business, and many ended up as greengrocers, as here in Little Bolivia. Others, less fortunate, were exploited as cheap household servants, workers in textile factories or laborers cultivating vegetables. Partly as a result of this discrimination, the Bolivian community in Buenos Aires has a strong identity and cohesion. They have arts centers and their own media. Officially about 350,000 Bolivians live in Argentina, but some estimates put the figure at closer to 1.5 million.

On Suárez and its side streets you can gain an impression of the lives of immigrants from the Andean lands. For example, on Ibarrola Street you can order a home-made Bolivian hotpot in the restaurant Miriam, and try *ceviche*, a typical Peruvian fish dish, on the floor above. The travel agency next door has the cheapest bus tickets to Cochabamba or La Paz, a journey that takes a mere 56 hours. Perhaps a trip out to Little Bolivia is enough for one day!

Address José León Suárez and streets running off it, between Av. Rivadavia and Ibarrola, Liniers, CABA | **Getting there** Sarmiento train line from Once to Liniers, or Subte A to San Pedrito, then bus 1, 2, 8, 136, or 163 | **Hours** Mon–Sat during the day | **Tip** Little Bolivia is halfway to the Museo Afro-Argentinos in Hurlingham (see ch. 68, the same train). The two can easily be combined in one trip.

62 Lo de Roberto

A tango dive

Buenos Aires is the city of tango. It is not easy to find your way through the dense jungle of *milongas* and *peñas* here, especially if you want to avoid the expensive shows that are solely arranged for tourists. To experience some truly authentic, pure, and honest tango, the place to go is a corner bar at the heart of Almagro, a traditional *barrio*.

Around 1930 there was a small grocery store here. Then Roberto Pérez opened a café that everyone called simply "Lo de Roberto" or "El Boliche de Roberto." When he died, a young new owner took it over, and made the wise decision to change nothing at all. He kept the surroundings and original character of this rough dive just as they were: the dusty collection of empty bottles bordering the dilapidated tiled roof, the worn-out chairs on an uneven chalk floor, and the ancient, bulky wooden refrigerator behind the bar, on which you can still see the hole made by a pistol bullet – traces of tough bygone days. The bar is cozy, dimly lit, and has a sense of community, just like the workers' drinking holes of the late 19th century, the years when tango was born.

You can immerse yourself in this world every evening, when tango and folk musicians perform with the bandoneon and guitar. Without a stage, without amplifiers, and impressively expressive, by candlelight they revive the original tango music of the 1920s, 1930s, and 1940s. If you enjoy their playing, you can put some money into the hat that is passed round later.

After midnight, if the great classics by Gardel and Pugliese are performed, the audience sing along, deeply moved, whatever their age, and when the bar owner himself, after a few glasses of wine, surprises guests with his deep, rich voice – then, if not earlier, you will come to the unshakeable conclusion that here you have found the most authentic of all locations for *tango porteño*.

Address Plaza Almagro, Bulnes 331, at the corner of General Juan Domingo Perón, Almagro, CABA | **Getting there** Subte B to Medrano; bus 19, 24, 26, 36, 71, 124, 127, 128, 151, 160, 168, or 180 | **Hours** Daily except Tue from 7pm, Sat, Sun sometimes opening later; from 10pm every table is often occupied | **Tip** More underground music: Tue–Sat tango, folklore, and jazz as well as good local food, round the corner at Cusca Risun (Perón 3649) sometimes with the same musicians, usually from 11pm (more information about the event on Facebook). Or refresh yourself for a long evening of tango with delicious vegetarian dishes at Curcuma (Sarmiento 3685, Tue–Sat 8pm–1am).

63 Luca Prodan's House

Remembering a rock hero

Jimi Hendrix, Kurt Cobain, and Sid Vicious – the names of exceptional musicians who died young after consuming drugs. In Argentina, this list is headed by the country's own tragic figure: Luca Prodan. Born in 1953 in Rome, in less than a decade he became the idol of the Argentinian rock scene. He was a cross between a chaotic gentleman and an educated punk, and to this day his voice sends a tingle down the spine of a whole generation.

Here, where he lived at the time of his death, this generation expresses its admiration. Lines from song lyrics and slogans such as "Luca not dead" are written, for preference in white correction fluid, on the old wooden doors of a working-class house dating from 1744. The house has become the memorial site for an artist who saw the emergence of punk rock in London in the 1970s and fell victim to heroin. To recover from drug use he came to Argentina, where he founded a band called Sumo and gave his first concert in Buenos Aires in 1981. The song lyrics in English were a thorn in the flesh of the military regime, which was at war with Britain about the Falkland Islands. When the war was lost and the military government too fell from power, Sumo provided the soundtrack for the emerging cultural revolution of the post-dictatorship period. But Luca did not survive this time in Buenos Aires. Clearly in bad health, he gave his last concert on December 20, 1987. Two days later, at just 34 years old, he died at home of cardiac arrest caused by cirrhosis of the liver. Twenty years later, fans opened the arts center La Casa de Luca in the house.

When asked whether Sumo could ever split up, Luca is said to have answered: "Sumo divididos? Las pelotas!" which means "Sumo split up? Never in a million years!" After his death, the other members of Sumo fell out and founded two new bands: Divididos and Las Pelotas.

Address Adolfo Alsina 451, Monserrat, CABA | **Getting there** Subte A to Plaza de Mayo, Subte E to Bolívar; bus 2, 8, 22, 24, 28, 29, 56, 64, 86, 91, 103, 105, 111, 126, or 143 | **Hours** Parties held at irregular intervals in La Casa de Luca Prodan are announced on Facebook and usually begin after midnight | **Tip** 12 *cuadras* away at the corner of Chacabuco and San Juan in San Telmo, the Sumo ice cream parlor is decorated with photos of the band (daily noon–midnight).

64 Mafalda and Co.

The circular route of the comic hero

It is almost impossible to get a photo of Mafalda. There is always someone pushing onto the bench to take a selfie next to this cheeky girl and her friends Susanita and Manolito. The statue of what is probably Argentina's most popular comic figure has long been an essential part of any guided tour of San Telmo. Most people, however, do not know that this is part of a trail on which you can make the acquaintance of many more heroes from comics of the last 80 years.

The 20 figures on the Paseo de la Historieta have all been placed in surroundings that suit them. For example, the bon viveur Isidoro Cañones, dating from 1935, is amidst bars on a street corner not far from Mafalda. She herself is seated, life-size, in front of her own house at Chile number 371, where a plaque at the entrance proclaims that "Mafalda lived here." In truth this was the home of her creator, the artist Quino. In 1964, he brought to life this girl who, for her age, is extremely thoughtful. From this time onwards Mafalda appeared in comic strips in various newspapers. She was constantly concerned about world peace and criticized the influence of the wealthy classes.

On the ground in front of her, a small sign points the way to the other cartoon characters on the trail. If you follow it to Balcarce Street, you will encounter the innocent, gullible Don Fulgencio, who along with his balloons is running away from becoming a grown-up. He was created in 1938 by Lino Palacio, and is the embodiment of the child that is in all of us. The Paseo de la Historieta then leads through the districts of San Telmo, Monserrat, and Puerto Madero, taking in several different decades of Argentinian comic history.

To read about Mafalda is to understand Argentina, it is said. And this surely also applies to the other heroes who have left the printed page and been cast in resin on this trail.

Address Mafalda: corner of Chile and Defensa. Don Fulgencio: Venezuela, corner of Balcarce, both in San Telmo, CABA | Getting there Subte C to Independencia; bus 22, 24, 28, 29, 86, 126, or 195 | Tip Fans of comics should end the trail in the Museo del Humor in Puerto Madero, a few meters from the last two figures, where there is an extensive collection of work by national comic artists (Av. de los Italianos 851, Mon–Fri 11am–6pm, Sat & Sun 10am–8pm, holidays noon–8pm).

65 Malvinas Park

Sense a claim to sovereignty

The Islas Malvinas, or Falkland Islands, in the South Atlantic have been a bone of contention between Argentina and the United Kingdom for more than 200 years. There are differing interpretations about who has sovereignty over the archipelago. In the 1770s, France, Britain, and Spain had bases on the islands. In 1776 the British withdrew, and the Spanish claim later passed to independent Argentina. In 1833 Britain retook the islands and named them the Falklands. An attempt by the Argentinian military regime to reconquer the islands failed miserably in the Falklands War of 1982. The residents see themselves as British, the United Nations categorizes the conflict as a long-term territorial dispute, and Argentina sticks to its claim that "The Malvinas are ours!"

A strange children's park and a museum in Buenos Aires are dedicated to this claim to sovereignty. The playground in the Parque de la Soberanía familiarizes children with the national point of view. They can climb and swing on penguins, sheep, and sea lions. Signs explain the role of these animals in the life of the islands. A huge Argentinian flag is reflected in the museum façade, and a model of the islands in a pond is intended to evoke a sense of the Atlantic. The big lighthouse that illuminates the neighboring highway at night also plays its part. The museum exhibit addresses the emotions: a film portrays the beauty, coldness, and emptiness of the Malvinas. This is intended to demonstrate to anyone with doubts that the islands are a geographical extension of Patagonia, and thus part of the Argentinian gaucho identity.

To be fair to the museum, it gives a balanced account of the Falklands War, but on its Facebook page a heated debate has broken out in which Argentinians, British people, and Kelpers – as the islanders are known – give voice to their views, sometimes respectfully, sometimes less so.

Address Espacio Memoria y Derechos Humanos (ex ESMA), Av. del Libertador 8151, Nuñez, CABA | **Getting there** Mitre train line from Retiro toward Tigre, to Rivadavia; bus 15, 28, 29, 117, or 130 | **Hours** Wed–Fri 9am–5pm, Sat, Sun, & holidays noon–8pm | **Tip** On the site of 'ex ESMA' is the former officers' mess, which was used as a torture center and is now a recommended museum about the history of the military dictatorship. The Casa por la Identidad (see ch. 24) is there.

66_Milestone No. 12

Citizens against the British Empire

What is it that constitutes Argentinian identity? In 2004, the band La Bersuit devoted a song to this difficult question.

In "La Argentinidad al Palo" they sang about the most beautiful women in the world, about superb football, and about many nations living together. But the lyrics also tell of dictatorships, poverty, and the economic crisis in 2001. This society of immigrants has always been preoccupied by the issue of what it means to be Argentinian. Yet the answer to this question – at least, if you refer to this monolith – is extremely simple: the roots of Argentinian national identity lie in the reconquest of the city from British forces in 1806 and 1807. A whole series of monuments is dedicated to these victories. They are numbered, and stand on the sites of the battles of those years.

For a long time, Britain had cast a covetous eye on the riches of South America. Industrialization and the rise of capitalism intensified the search for new markets. In order to prevent the French from taking control of Latin America during the Napoleonic Wars, the British army took possession of Buenos Aires in June 1806. The Spanish viceroy, Marquis Rafael de Sobremonte, fled to Córdoba, and *The Times* proudly announced that the city now belonged to the British Empire. But only 46 days later, the local militia, strongly supported by the population, drove out the invaders. On the spot where these events took place, the weathered 'milestone of Argentinidad no. 12' commemorates the victory.

When a second attempt in 1807 also ended in disaster, Britain had to give up its ambitions in the region once and for all. The local elites felt that their mother country, Spain, had left them in the lurch, and the victory over British forces bolstered their self-confidence – an important factor in the lead-up to the May Revolution of 1810 that ultimately contributed to independence.

Address Plaza San Martín, Maipú between Av. Santa Fé and Arenales, Retiro, CABA | **Getting there** Subte C to San Martín; bus 6, 7, 9, 20, 22, 23, 26, 28, 33, 45, and others | **Tip** Four *cuadras* further on, at the corner of Suipacha and Arroyo, a square commemorates the bombing of the Israeli Embassy, which stood here, in 1992.

67 The MOB Building

Homage to Evita and corruption

This functional, 93-meter-high building has changed the urban landscape of Buenos Aires twice. Shortly after its completion in 1936, it became clear that a planning failure had happened: construction of a wide north-side road in the city center had been decided a long time previously, but the Ministerio de Obras Públicas (MOB) stood in the way at the south end of the planned expressway. There were several proposals for how to avoid pulling down the new building. One was to remove the walls of the ground floor and let the cars drive through. But the idea that gained most support was to build an identical skyscraper at the north end, and thus create two gateways for the monumental new thoroughfare. The second tower was never constructed, but the MOB Building survived, and became, alongside the obelisk, the second emblem of the new Avenida 9 de Julio.

As the other buildings on the avenida lie on smaller parallel roads that have their own names, this is the only one with the official address 9 de Julio 1925.

In 2011, the building once again transformed the character of the city center. The Kirchner government had two steel images of Eva Perón attached to it: toward Constitución a smiling Evita, an elegant representative of the state, and on the north side the militant revolutionary at a microphone. This had symbolic importance, as in August 1951, from the balcony of this building, the first lady announced to cheering supporters, that she would stand for the office of vice-president. This never took place, as she died the following July.

The two Art Deco figures on the eastern corners of the high-rise are also noteworthy. One of them is holding a suitcase, and the other is furtively holding a hand open behind his back. They are said to symbolize corruption – on a ministry building? This interpretation has never been officially confirmed, but it is the obvious answer.

Address Av. 9 de Julio 1925, corner of Moreno and Monserrat, CABA | Getting there Subte C to Moreno; bus 8, 9, 10, 17, 45, 56, 59, 64, 67, 70, and others | Hours Viewable from the outside only | Tip From here, walk five *cuadras* to the traditional restaurant Plaza Mayor and its outstanding Spanish food (Venezuela 1399, daily noon–1am).

68__The Museo Afro-Argentino

In search of African roots

Argentina feels it is a European country. For a long time there was no place for African origins in public discourse. For decades, historians and politicians maintained that there were no blacks in Argentina, and that the small number of slaves – in reality there were significantly more – had died in wars or through disease, or had emigrated. Neither are the immigrants who came to Buenos Aires from the Cape Verde islands in the 19th century mentioned in any schoolbook. This version of history is now being disputed with increasing vehemence.

One voice that has been raised in this cause is that of the Institute for Research and Dissemination of Black Cultures. Most of its members are white Argentinians who have found their spiritual home in the Afro-Brazilian Candomblé religion, But they show considerable commitment. In the 1980s they founded the Museo Afro-Argentino in their temple in Buenos Aires Province. The aim is to show the "soul of the cultures of Africa" here, with masks, cult items, and traditional robes. The emphasis is more on the spiritual roots of Candomblé in West Africa than on the current political and social situation of Afro-Argentinos. It is worth paying a visit to the museum if only because the leaders of the community are most willing to provide information about their religion, which is widely practiced in Brazil. More general questions about the life of Afro-Argentinos are handled by the institute by means of scholarly congresses, which it has already organized four times in collaboration with the national library. Here, discussions were held about a study recently published by the University of Buenos Aires, which concluded that approximately two million Argentinians have black ancestors. The saying "Argentinians come from the boats" is true – but not all of the boats sailed there from Europe!

Address Húsares 476, Villa Tesei, Hurlingham, Provincia | **Getting there** Sarmiento train line from Once to Morón, then bus 443, 463, or taxi | **Hours** Irregular, for inquiries +11/4450-4586 or see www.doyo.com.ar/home/contacto | **Tip** If you are interested in the subject but do not want to make this journey, visit the Movimiento Afrocultural arts center in San Telmo (Defensa 535).

69 The Museo del Agua

Or: the water closet museum

The main exhibits in this museum, which is devoted to the history of water supply, are toilet bowls. Hundreds of urinals and water closets in all shapes and sizes can be admired here. The museum is housed in the Palacio de Aguas Corrientes, an imposing building dating from 1894 that belongs to the municipal utility company. Over 350,000 pieces of terracotta were imported from London for its façade in the eclectic style. Within it are 12 cisterns with a total volume of some 72 million liters of water. The tanks were built to improve hygienic conditions in the fast-growing city. Plague, typhus, and cholera were virulent in Buenos Aires at the beginning of the 19th century.

Later, the same building accommodated the department responsible for inspecting the quality of toilets. As there was no norm for this at that time, companies had to make one sample of all their own and imported models available for a functional test. They had names like Iris, Superbus, Eterna, or Strong. To examine flow through the drainage pipe, the porcelain bowls were cut through in the middle. The museum still possesses a few examples of these halved toilets. Apart from this, a varied array of taps, pieces of pipe, water meters, and toilet cisterns tells the eventful story of the progress of sanitation – not only in Argentina. This exhibition is framed by furnishings from the days when the WC testers went about their business.

An obvious question is, why is such a splendid building needed to cover up a few cisterns (which, by the way, can also be visited)? The population was not aware of the benefits of the water supply, as this produced long-lasting building works that were literally a drain on public finances. And when it was all completed, you could not even see where the money had gone. The purpose of the Palacio de Aguas was to make the value of the system visible to all.

Address Palacio de Aguas, Riobamba 750, Balvanera, CABA | **Getting there** Subte D to Callao; bus 12, 29, 37, 60, 75, 99, 106, 109, 111, 124, 132, 140, or 150 | **Hours** Mon–Fri 9am–1pm | **Tip** On a plaza two *cuadras* further along Av. Santa Fé, at the corner of Junín, stands a huge building of the Faculty of Medicine in Brutalist style. It is a stark contrast to the magnificent building that houses this museum.

70_The Narrowest House

2.5 meters for a freed slave

San Telmo is undoubtedly the best quarter of the city for going in search of old Buenos Aires. Most of the buildings date from the 19th century and are protected monuments. Every one of them has an interesting story to tell, and among these, Casa Mínima is particularly unusual.

In Pasaje San Lorenzo, only 50 meters from Defensa, the main tourist street of San Telmo, stands the house with the city's narrowest front, Casa Mínima. Various sources agree that one of the first freed slaves lived here. Buenos Aires was one of the biggest slave markets in the Americas. The first people who were forcibly taken from West Africa were bought and sold here from 1580 onwards. In the 17th century this trade flourished in Argentina, as slaves were increasingly used as laborers in animal husbandry. A census carried out in 1810 categorized the inhabitants of Buenos Aires as 22,793 whites, 9,615 blacks, and 150 indigenous persons.

After the prohibition of the trade in Argentina in 1812, former slaves were entitled to a place to live – though a small one. This pretty little building, with its miniscule balcony, is said to have been built personally by a *liberto*, as freed slaves were called. According to a different version of the story, the former slave owner simply separated off part of his own house and made it available to a freed slave, after whose death the casita passed back to the original owner. Whatever the truth of the matter, it is less than two-and-a-half meters wide, but goes back 13 meters from the road. The brick façade that has been revealed on the upper part of the building shows that it has a long history.

The next but one building awaits restoration to save it from final ruin. It is known to be one of the oldest in Buenos Aires. There are conflicting opinions about whether it is truly the very oldest building, as some people believe.

Address Pasaje San Lorenzo 380, San Telmo, CABA | **Getting there** Subte C and E to Independencia; bus 22, 24, 28, 29, 86, 126, or 195 | **Tip** El Desnivel around the corner is one of the best *parrillas* (grill restaurants) in Buenos Aires (Defensa 855, Mon 7pm–1am, Tue–Sat noon–1am, Sun noon–midnight).

71 The National Library

From another era

The massive bulk of the reading room of the National Library in Recoleta rises above its narrower, but scarcely more elegant base. Unadorned, the clear geometrical forms of its rough reinforced concrete protrude, lending the building a futuristic appearance, especially at night.

It is an overwhelming embodiment of the international Brutalist architectural movement of the 1960s. The name of the style is derived from the French term *béton brut*, raw concrete. And this material was used lavishly. According to the Magna Carta of this architectural style, buildings were supposed to concentrate entirely on their function. The readers in this library have an unobstructed view across the harbor, while the books were banished to subterranean stacks.

Ironically, the golden age of Brutalism had long passed when the library was opened in 1992. No less a person than the writer Jorge Luis Borges, then director of the library, had begun planning the new building as long ago as the late 1950s, but the foundation stone was not laid until 1971. Construction was continually delayed, and then suspended during the last military dictatorship. When work resumed in 1982, the requirements placed on a modern library had radically changed, and 10 further years passed before it was completed.

This makes the national library not only a good example of the delays experienced by public construction projects in Argentina, but also a witness to the turbulent history of the country: shortly after independence it was founded by Mariano Moreno, after whom it is named, and initially held the book collections of the Jesuit order. In its present location it stands exactly on the site of the residence of Juan Perón and Evita. This land became available when the military destroyed the president's house in 1955, bombarded Plaza de Mayo, and finally drove Perón from office through their coup.

Address Agüero 2502, Recoleta, CABA | Getting there Bus 10, 37, 41, 59, 60, 61, 62, 67, 92, 93, and others | Hours Mon–Fri 7am–midnight, Sat & Sun noon–7pm, admission only with a library pass, public tours in Spanish Mon–Fri 4pm | Tip Behind the library stands a statue of Pope John Paul II, here walking on water. It was donated by the city's Polish community.

72_The Orange Courtyard

A colonial oasis in the Centro Cultural Recoleta

Although Buenos Aires has many lovely parks, sometimes you long for a tranquil place where you can switch off amongst all the noise of the city. At the heart of vibrant Recoleta lies a hidden oasis in the colonial style: the Patio de los Naranjos in the Centro Cultural Recoleta. Even though some of them no longer bear fruit, the small citrus trees are enchantingly beautiful in this colonial setting. They are an invitation to bring along a good book and take a deep breath.

Some 20 trees are surrounded by chalk-white walls and red tiled roofs that belong to one of the oldest surviving buildings in the city. Originally this was the site of a monastery of Franciscan monks, completed in 1732. This part of the city owes its name to them. The Convento de Recoletos Descalzos also built a small church and established the well-known Recoleta cemetery here. However, as the monks, who were born in Spain, resisted the first independent Argentinian government following the May Revolution of 1810, they were banished to the remote province of Catamarca. After that the complex was used successively as a school, a barracks, a prison, an old persons' home, and a botanical garden.

The Courtyard of Oranges appears to be a relic of this last role. It can be visited at all times when the arts center, which has been housed here since 1980, is open. It is the first of four courtyards situated on the left after you pass through the entrance. With a little luck, you will visit when the orange trees are in blossom, normally the period from February to May and from July to August. Then a particularly strong scent fills the courtyard.

It is also well worth visiting the other three patios. The Patio de la Fuente, or Fountain Court, is often used for exhibitions. The arts center also runs guided tours on themes connected to the history of the building.

Address Junín 1930, Recoleta, CABA | **Getting there** Bus 17, 61, 62, 67, 92, 93, 110, 124, or 130 | **Hours** Tue–Fri 1:30–10pm, Sat, Sun, & holidays 11:30am–10pm; information on tours at www.centroculturalrecoleta.org | **Tip** Near the arts center is the Museo Nacional de Bellas Artes (Av. del Libertador 1473, Tue–Fri 11am–8pm, Sat & Sun 10am–8pm).

73__Palacio Barolo

Dante Alighieri everywhere you look

Luis Barolo was a progressive thinker and a successful businessman who came to Buenos Aires from Italy in 1890. After World War I, he expected the complete destruction of European culture. In collaboration with his compatriot Mario Palanti, a renowned architect, he therefore wanted to commemorate it. They designed the Palacio Barolo, a pioneering office building.

As Italians, they were above all concerned that Dante Alighieri's *Divine Comedy* might be buried beneath the ruins of a new war and be lost to human memory. They therefore included many references to the work on their building on Avenida de Mayo. Like Dante's masterpiece, it is divided into three parts: hell, purgatory, and paradise. The lobby is ornamented with Latin inscriptions. The nine entrances represent the nine circles of hell, while the lighthouse at the tip of the tower stands for the choirs of angels. The total height of the building, 100 meters, corresponds to the hundred songs in Dante's work, the 22 stories to its 22 verses. Architecturally, the building combines Gothic Revival and Romantic elements. The dome was inspired by a Hindu temple and symbolizes the union of Dante and his deceased lover. These are only the obvious details. Beyond that, there are a number of metaphorical refinements that relate to Dante. The Palacio Barolo was opened in 1923 on – surprise, surprise! – the poet's birthday.

In addition to the 11 official elevators, the building is also equipped with two secret elevators. Barolo used them to reach his offices on the first and second floors without being bothered by his tenants. It is said that the rays emanating from the lighthouse can be seen as far away as Uruguay. There, in Montevideo, stands a well-known twin of the Palacio Barolo. Constructed a short time later by the same architect, the Palacio Salvo became the most important landmark in the Uruguayan capital.

Address Av. de Mayo 1370, Monserrat, CABA | Getting there Subte A to Sáenz Peña; bus 8, 23, 39, 56, 60, 64, 86, 102, 105, 151, or 168 | Hours Mon–Fri noon–8pm, day and night tours incl. 360-degree view of the city: www.palaciobarolotours.com.ar | Tip One *cuadra* away in front of the Congress building is the monolith from which all distances in Argentina are measured. It is guarded by the patron saint of roads, Nuestra Señora de Luján.

74_The Panamericana

From Alaska to Tierra del Fuego via Buenos Aires

A trip in a campervan along the Panamericana from Alaska to Tierra del Fuego: for decades this has been the dream of many road-trip adventurers. But, not to put too fine a point on it, this just isn't possible. For one thing, between Panama and Colombia the Panamericana is interrupted for a distance of about 90 kilometers. The rainforest there is so incalculable that there is nothing for it but to take an alternate route by air or water. For another thing, officially the world's most famous highway only runs from Buenos Aires to Mexico. All other parts of the route, for example the Alaska Highway, which is popularly known as *the* Panamericana, have been unofficially added for tourist purposes.

Many *porteños* do not know that the 17-lane highway that branches off from the General Paz orbital highway in the north of Buenos Aires really is *the* Panamericana. Most people assume that this is only a nickname derived from its width. But Ruta 9, as it is called in the national road network, is the official start of this transcontinental express road, which was initiated in 1923 by the states of the Americas. If you keep driving straight ahead from here, you will reach Mexico – 14 states, one ferry trip, and many altitude and climatic zones later. Nevertheless, you should have a road map at your elbow, as there is no standard signage on the Panamericana.

With its length of 25,750 kilometers, taking the most extensive north-south link, it is the main artery of the Americas. These dimensions are reflected in the part of the route that passes through Buenos Aires: here the Panamericana is flanked by the biggest shopping malls, movie theaters, short-stay hotels, and steakhouses. Moreover, all long-distance buses that go to central or northern Argentina leave the city on the Panamericana. The longest bus journey that you can book in Argentina, by the way, goes to Lima in Peru.

Address Autopista Pascual Palazzo, Ruta 9, from Av. General Paz in Vicente López, Provincia | **Getting there** The routes of buses 15, 60, 228, and 430, for example, partly run on the Panamericana | **Tip** For hard-core shoppers, the Unicenter near the Panamericana is Argentina's biggest shopping center and one of the 10 largest in South America (Av. Paraná 3745, Martínez, Provincia).

75_Parque Avellaneda

History and culture in the city's loveliest park

The history of Parque Avellaneda begins with a community of nuns who ran an orphanage and cultivated a garden for medicinal herbs here, 10 kilometers from Plaza de Mayo, in the 17th century. The name of this place, Chacra de los Remedios (farm of the healing herbs), derives from the nunnery garden. As part of a church reform in the 1820s, the area was confiscated and sold to the Olivera family, who established an independent agricultural research laboratory and built a beautiful villa in the eclectic style. In 1912, the family sold its country estate to the city authorities, who eventually declared it a public park.

When communal life ground to a halt during the last military dictatorship, the estate fell into a condition of visible neglect. After the return to democracy in the 1980s, people from the neighborhood took care of the park. Since then its fate has been determined by an unprecedented commission representing both the state and civil society.

Far away from the beaten tourist track, the 26-hectare Parque Avellaneda is probably the most beautiful park in Buenos Aires today. This is not only a place to enjoy the extensive natural grassland – the trip is also worthwhile for the historic buildings. Recently, the old miniature railway (a locomotive and four cars) has come back into service. It used to chug around the zoological garden in Palermo. The old swimming pool in Art Nouveau style is an especially fine sight. Built in 1923, it was the first public pool in Buenos Aires. Today, the pupils of the Ernesto Che Guevara middle school use its tiled basin as their playground during breaks.

The remaining buildings have been made over to the Chacra de los Remedios arts center. More than 20 different workshops are regularly held here. Every weekend, performances take place in the open air. The villa of the Olivera family now houses a center for contemporary art.

Address Parque Presidente Nicolás Avellaneda, corner of Av. Directorio and Av. Lacarra, Parque Avellaneda, CABA | **Getting there** Subte E to Plaza de los Virreyes, then about 10 minutes' walk; bus 4, 5, 7, 36, 46, 49, 50, 55, 56, 86, and others | **Hours** Daily in daylight hours; events in the arts center mainly on weekends, see www.facebook.com/chacra.remedios | **Tip** Combine the visit with the Feria de Mataderos (see ch. 41) or the secret prison Ex CCDTyE Olimpo (see ch. 38), which also lie outside the city center.

76 Parque Chas

Small, new, confusing

Buenos Aires was laid out in the typical grid plan of a former Spanish colony. The district of Parque Chas in the north-west of the city diverges from this pattern so strongly, however, that it is generally regarded as a taxi driver's nightmare. It was planned in concentric circles, with a few roads cutting through them laterally. If you drive in, it is difficult to find your way out again, because for *porteños* who are used to finding their way according to *cuadras*, this departure from the norm is quite a challenge. Even for the inhabitants of the labyrinth it is difficult to explain how to get from A to B. But when you take a stroll through this picturesque *barrio*, there is one guiding rule: the unending circular roads are named for European cities such as London, Berlin, and Cádiz. Those that lead out of the maze have the names of people.

The eponymous Chas family are to blame for this failure of orientation. They were big landlords who had several estates around the old city center. A third-generation son wanted to sell the land in about 1925. To make the new district more attractive, he divided it up into plots as usual, but laid out the blocks in these unaccustomed circular shapes. "Unique in South America," his advertising slogan proclaimed.

For a few years, Parque Chas belonged to the Agronomía district. With its area of 1.4 square kilometers it regained its independence in 2005. This makes it not only the most unusual, but also the most recent and the smallest of the 48 *barrios* of Buenos Aires. Its unique shape and history have given rise to a distinctive district identity. A private house is home to a neighborhood center, Puerta de los Gatos, organized by the citizens themselves.

For the 90th anniversary of Parque Chas in 2015, the residents held several street parties. They are proud of their role as outsiders in the city.

Address Between Av. Triunvirato, Av. de los Incas, Andonaegui and La Pampa, Parque Chas, CABA | **Getting there** Subte B to De Los Incas – Parque Chas; bus 80, 87, 108, 111, 123, or 127 | **Hours** For events in the quarter: www.facebook.com/ParqueChasWeb | **Tip** You can easily combine a visit to Parque Chas on foot with the Agriculture Faculty (see ch. 3).

77 Pasaje Lanín

The artist's work is his street

When the artist Marino Santa María painted his own house in an abstract design in 2001, the result inspired him to do more. He photographed the neighboring houses and redesigned their façades, too – only digitally at first. When he proposed turning the digital idea into analog reality, the residents were initially skeptical, and it took the artist a long time to win them round to the suggestion. Unbelievable as it may be, today all of his neighbors are proud of their quiet street, Pasaje Lanín: 40 out of 43 houses are resplendent in vivid colors. The walls are now dominated by an interplay of various primary colors, always in harmony with the original style of the house façade.

Santa María wanted to create neither an open-air museum nor an overcrowded pedestrian zone like the touristy Caminito in La Boca, as he said when he set the project of painted façades rolling with a street party on April 19, 2001. He envisioned a large work of art that permanently changes and evolves.

Keeping his word, in 2005 he took the project into its next phase by placing Venetian mosaic tiles on the walls, yet without changing the original shapes and colors of the works. Marino Santa María does not deny that the result is something like a fusion of Hundertwasser and Gaudí.

If you take a stroll along Pasaje Lanín, you will find Marino in his studio at number 33. He always leaves the door wide open. He exhibits his works here, and is pleased to talk about the art project. He also holds workshops on painting and mosaic art. His intention is that Pasaje Lanín should create a connection between everyday life and art, and thus make it accessible for everybody, without having to go to an art gallery or museum. Marino has achieved this aim. You just have to seek it out in the Barracas district, where it lies hidden between the rail tracks and the highway.

Address Lanín 1-200, Barracas, CABA, www.marinosantamaria.com | Getting there Bus 25, 45, 51, 79, 95, 100, 134, 148, or 195 | Tip Another installation by this artist, Huellas del Aire, adorns the railway wall.

78_Pasaje Rivarola

Mirror symmetry

As soon as you enter Pasaje Rodolfo Rivarola, your clone appears on the sidewalk opposite. When you leave it at the other end, the clone disappears. This is the gist of a legend about this short, 100-meter street in the city center. It is as if someone had placed a mirror in the middle. On each side stand four buildings, with three apartments on each of five floors. They form completely identical and seamless façades from one end of the street to the other. Each of the four corner buildings is crowned by a dome with a view. The doors, the decorations on the balcony balustrades, the details of the façade: absolutely everything is symmetrical.

This obsession with symmetry derives from the architectural practice Petersen, Thiele y Cruz, which still exists. They were commissioned by an insurance company to design the buildings, street, and sidewalks between 1924 and 1926. Typically for that time, the style reveals the inspiration of Parisian architecture. The unique charm of this *pasaje*, as streets are called when they are only one *cuadra* (block) long, makes it an oasis of peace, quite different from the noisy chaos that surrounds it. A lot of intellectuals have made it their home, but only those who can afford to pay rents that are well above the average. The middle-class aura that distinguishes the street has made it the backdrop for cinema movies and advertisements on a number of occasions.

The characteristic clock on number 134 is a perfect fit for the aesthetics of Pasaje Rodolfo Rivarola. For decades it adorned the Casa Raab watchmaker's store, but since the death of the owner, Miguel Raab, it has stood still. Raab only repaired clocks and watches that were made in the 1950s or earlier.

If the Harry Potter movies had been made in Buenos Aires, the watchmaker Raab would have been the ideal setting for Ollivander's magic wand store.

Address Between Gral. Juan Domingo Perón and Bartolomé Mitre at no. 1300, San Nicolás, CABA | **Getting there** Subte A to Sáenz Peña, or Subte B to Uruguay; bus 6, 7, 9, 10, 17, 24, 26, 29, 45, 50, and others | **Tip** At number 147 is the women's museum, dedicated to female cultural and art history (Tue–Sat 3–8pm).

79_Pejerrey Fishermen's Club

A saltwater bath at Quilmes

It would be the perfect setting for a horror film: decaying pavilions, wooden buildings full of cracks, and rotten boards through which you fall into the waters of the Río de la Plata when fleeing from the chain-saw murderer. The broad pier of the Pejerrey fishermen's club in Quilmes has seen better days, but you can still sense the high-class atmosphere that once surrounded the waterside here. In 1927, an Italian family opened this leisure park, with Argentina's first swimming pool integrated into the pier. It was filled with saltwater that had been discovered by drilling 70 meters beneath the ground. The rambla on wooden piles became a popular spot for day trippers from the city. Those who could not afford a holiday on the beach in Mar del Plata had a refreshing alternative in Quilmes.

In 1938, the fishermen's club was founded and later took over the whole site. In the 1950s its members built the anglers' pier that stretches 700 meters out into the river. Over the years, weathering has taken its toll on the boards, and much of the pier is no longer safe. Financial support from the state for restoration never reached the club. Since November 2015, Quilmes has had a new mayor, and the club committee hopes once again that the original spirit of the pier can still be saved.

The two pools with their turquoise water, by contrast, have retained their Caribbean charm. You might think that the bottom of the pool had been painted in that color, and some people think the water is polluted with algae. But neither of these things is true: the saltwater comes straight from the depths of the earth and is changed every three days. This is a stroke of luck for the Quilmeños, as the river long ago ceased to be fit for swimming. After splashing around in the water, you can sunbathe and have a cold beer – a Quilmes, of course.

Address Av. Cervantes, corner of Av. Isidoro G. Iriarte, Quilmes, Provincia | **Getting there** Roca train line from Constitución with destination La Plata or Bosques to Quilmes, then bus 278, 281, 585, or taxi. Alternatives: buses 85 (from Flores, Caballito) and 98 (from Once via Constitución) stop at the entrance to the club. | **Hours** Pier and swimming pool open to non-members daily except Tue 10am–7pm, anglers' pier and park always open | **Tip** There are two larger restaurants where you can enjoy the river scene, even in winter – perhaps for fresh fish?

80 Plaza de Mayo

Palm trees, ducks, and a missing church tower

Hardly anyone visits Buenos Aires without coming to Plaza de Mayo. It is the political and historical center of Argentina. The Cabildo, Casa Rosada, national bank, and main cathedral are here, one representation of power next to another. The oldest square in the country is the setting for countless strange stories that are not found in the guidebooks. Here are a few of them.

In 1610, the plaza was a popular sports ground. When playing the traditional game of *pato*, two teams of riders tried to capture a living duck. Today this game, with its similarity to polo, has become a national sport, but the duck is now made from leather.

The palm trees that embellish the square were brought from Río de Janeiro in the 19th century. A heated debate broke out in the city about whether they would survive the climate of Buenos Aires. More than 100 years have passed since then, and the optimists have won the argument. The trees were endangered only during the economic crisis of 2001, when some of them were set alight by angry demonstrators.

The white pyramid in the middle was originally only half as tall. When it was erected in 1811 on the first anniversary of the May Revolution, it was only 15 meters high. This was not enough for a symbol of freedom, it was decided 40 years later, so an addition with the female figure was simply placed on top.

Beneath this pyramid, the Madres de la Plaza de Mayo protested during the military dictatorship against the disappearance of their children. In 1977, a policeman told them they could not stand there. They took him at his word, and from that time they walked round and round the monument. The painted circle with its symbols of headscarves stands for their struggle and legendary circuits of the pyramid.

Last but not least: the cathedral once had a tower. The remaining stump stands to the left of the entrance. So keep your eyes open!

Address Plaza de Mayo, between Av. Rivadavia, Bolívar, Hipólito Yrigoyen, and Balcarce, Monserrat, CABA | **Getting there** Subte A to Plaza de Mayo, Subte D to Catedral, Subte E to Bolívar; bus 22, 24, 28, 29, 56, 61, 62, 64, 74, 86, and others | **Tip** This book presents three more unusual places around Plaza de Mayo (see ch. 10, 15, & 49).

81 Plaza Pappo

A monument to Mr. Cheese

Countless streets, monuments, and squares in and around Buenos Aires are dedicated to former President Roque Sáenz Peña (1851–1914). So this plaza in Villa Mitre is just one more, and doesn't make much difference, does it? Since a monument was erected here for the deceased rock guitarist Norberto Napolitano, his fans have been campaigning for the park to be renamed Plaza Pappo. In preparation for this event, they have already sprayed over the signs. Everyone knew this man with long hair and a prominent chin as "Pappo," short for El Carpo, the wrist. His virtuosity at extracting from the guitar sounds that had never been heard before was responsible for the nickname. Pappo is regarded as one of the founders of Rock Nacional and Blues Argentino in the 1960s. He was also the first musician to bring heavy metal to Argentina. In the course of his career, he played in several bands, the best-known of which was Pappo's Blues, with whom he recorded a total of nine studio albums.

Guitars were the love of his life, so it is no wonder that the monument in his honor depicts Pappo with a guitar, and that its base is adorned with hundreds of his plectrums. A plaque bears his famous line of lyrics: "When you no longer feel the caresses of my hands and the warmth of my body, then, guitar, you will weep!" Argentinian bands such as Los Piojos and Almafuerte paid for the monument. Pappo also had international admirers, including no less a person that the blues legend B. B. King, who simply called him "Mr Cheese." King could never forget that Pappo had presented him with a cheese at their first meeting.

On February 25, 2005 Pappo fell from his Harley-Davidson near Luján and was run over by a car coming from the opposite direction. A procession of fans and bikers, singing, and cheering, accompanied his funeral cortege to the Chacarita Cemetery (see ch. 26).

Address Plaza Roque Sáenz Peña, corner of Juan B. Justo and Andrés Lamas, Villa General Mitre, CABA | **Getting there** Subte A to Carabobo, then bus 113, or the San Martín train line from Retiro via Palermo to La Paternal, then bus 44; bus 34, 44, 110, 113, or 166 | **Hours** Accessible 24 hours | **Tip** Football fans should go four *cuadras* to see the Diego Armando Maradona stadium of the Argentino Juniors (Av. Boyacá and San Blas), where Maradona played his first professional match in 1976.

82 Puente de los Carros

An inspiration, symbol, and film setting

In the early 20th century there was a widely held delusion in Buenos Aires that the steam from locomotives was a remedy for breathing difficulties. This bridge, which is on the border between Constitución and Barracas, is said to have been a place to which parents liked to take their sick children to hold them over the parapet when a train rattled past beneath. But not only its function as a supposed fresh-air sanatorium has made the bridge, built in 1927, the unofficial emblem of the two districts. It is also a particularly fine example of railway architecture, which came here from Liverpool. Several solid steel girders make it seem like a kind of tunnel. Before it was built, there was only a temporary crossing of the tracks that connected the Constitución terminus with the southern suburbs. Its construction enabled cars and a tram to cross, earning it the plain nickname Puente de los Carros.

A famous fan even dedicated the opening lines of a poem to the bridge. In *Mateo XXV, 30*, Jorge Luis Borges wrote: "The first Constitution bridge, and at my feet the thundering of the trains that wove iron labyrinths. Smoke and whistles scaled the night, suddenly was the Universal Judgment." Borges loved to roam through the remote areas of his home town, and he often ended up at this hidden bridge.

Apart from some smears of graffiti, Puente de los Carros looks as good almost 100 years on as it did when it first opened. The cobblestones, arranged in a semi-circular pattern, have survived, and so have the embedded rails of the tram line that once passed through. When a proposal was made to demolish parts of the bridge in 2009, some local residents protested, and in the end it was granted heritage status. The bridge has repeatedly been used as a backdrop for movies, most recently in *The Colony* starring Daniel Brühl and Emma Watson.

Address Ituzaingó between Paracas and Guanahani, Barracas and Constitución, CABA | **Getting there** Subte C to Constitución; bus 25, 45, 51, 79, 95, 100, 102, 134, 148, 154, 168, or 195 | **Tip** Don't fail to take a photo of the old tango joint that is on the verge of collapse at the corner of Guanahani. The atmosphere must have been fantastic!

83 Pueyrredón Farm

A neglected historical gem

When Chacra Pueyrredón was built in 1830, Buenos Aires had only 60,000 inhabitants. Out here, far from the city center, big landowners had extensive farms. Only a few of these *chacras* have survived the ravages of time. The plots were concreted over long ago.

It is surreal: in the middle of Villa Ballester, a typical suburb with high-rises and a pedestrian zone, you chance upon the well-preserved Chacra Pueyrredón. Apart from visits by schoolchildren, it is invisible on the tourist map of Buenos Aires. What a pity! This house in the colonial style with its dovecote and stables is an impressive illustration of rural life in the 19th century.

Moreover, it is a significant historical site: when the British invaded Buenos Aires in 1806 (see ch. 32 and 66), they had one of their few successes in the Battle of Predriel. Later, in 1834, the journalist José Hernández was born here. He was a gifted analyst of the times he lived in. Nobody in Argentina leaves school without reading his epic poem "El Gaucho Martín Fierro," written in 1872. It is an outcry against the oligarchy of big landowners and a plea for a world with greater social justice. Martín Fierro, more than any other work of literature, plays a part in defining the identity of Argentina.

By the way, the name of this *chacra* was not borrowed from the famous General Pueyrredón, but from Victoria and Mariano Pueyrredón, a married couple who lived here. However, they were all descendants of one French merchant who arrived at the Río de la Plata in 1764. Today, the original Pueyrredón has 18,000 descendants. In 2000, what was probably the biggest family get-together of all time took place: 2,000 Pueyrredóns met in Pilar. In 1959, the last member of the family who lived in this *chacra* made it over to the Buenos Aires Provincia, which dedicated a museum to José Hernandez on the premises.

Address Presbítero Carballo 5042, Villa Ballester, General San Martín, Provincia | **Getting there** Mitre train line in the direction of Suárez to San Martín, then bus 169, 176, 310, or 670 to Ruta 8, at the corner of General Roca (opposite the YPF filling station), past the police station, two *cuadras* on from Lacroze (Subte B) take bus 176 or from Congreso de Tucumán (Subte D) bus 169 | **Hours** Mon–Fri 8am–3pm | **Tip** About 20 *cuadras* from here, in the center of Villa Ballester, stands a Gothic Revival church. To get there, call a taxi from the museum. Return with the Mitre train from Ballester.

84 Quinta Los Ombúes

400 years of high society

The surroundings of this picturesque country house have nothing to do with the Buenos Aires that visitors normally see. In the middle of a romantic park, it lies on a hill in San Isidro with a stunning view of the Río de la Plata. Visiting Quinta Los Ombúes is a stark contrast to La Boca or the Conventillo de la Paloma (see ch. 31). While slaves from Africa, and later immigrants from Europe, labored in the city center and the docks, here generations of important landowners, politicians, and business people enjoyed a life of indulgence.

It all began when the Spanish navigator and colonist Juan de Garay divided the land on the north bank of the river among his followers. After founding Buenos Aires for the second time in 1580, he drew perfectly straight lines on the map, creating rectangular-shaped estates from the shore to the interior. This *quinta* occupied plot number 57. In the following 400 years, the high society of Buenos Aires moved in and out of here. The estate changed hands many times, and the first house was built here in the mid-18th century. Leading figures in Argentinian history, for example José de San Martín, Juan Martín de Pueyrredón, and Manuel Belgrano, visited the quinta.

The last owners were members of the Beccar Varela family, who acquired the *quinta* in 1881. Following the fashion of the times, in 1925 one of the heirs remodeled the courtyard in the style of a Mediterranean patio with columns and Andalucian tiles. In his will, he laid down that the *quinta* would pass to the local municipality when his last child died. This happened in 2005: the commune of San Isidro restored the villa and opened a museum there.

There is really no better place to trace the history of the rich and powerful families of Buenos Aires. On one of the walls you can see a copy of the map with Juan de Garay's divisions of the land into estates.

Address Beccar Varela 774, San Isidro, Provincia | **Getting there** Mitre train line from Retiro toward Mitre to Olivos, then change to Tren de la Costa to San Isidro, or Mitre train from Retiro toward Tigre to San Isidro and walk about 10 minutes to the river; bus 168 toward San Isidro | **Hours** Apr–Oct Tue & Thu 10am–6pm, Sat & Sun 2–6pm, Nov–Mar Tue & Thu 10am–6pm, Sat & Sun 3–7pm, guided tour of the garden once a month | **Tip** Behind the quinta stands an impressive church dating from 1898, with a craft market in front of it every weekend.

85 The Red Riding Hood Monument

Grimm's fairy tales in the woods of Palermo

Some Argentinians like to make fun of the German language, using a stiff pronunciation and ending every word, whatever it is, with "en." A few years ago, a comedian told his own version of the fairy tale of Little Red Riding Hood and the big bad wolf. In this television sketch, his parody of German made "Caperucita Roja" into "Caperuciten Rojen." Even though this ancient story probably did not originate in Germany, but was written down for the first time in 1695 by the French author Charles Perrault, it was the Brothers Grimm who made it famous and gave it a happy end. They added the hunter, who liberated Red Riding Hood and her grandmother by cutting open the wolf's stomach and filling it with stones, causing him to collapse and die.

Generations of children on the Río de la Plata have grown up learning the Brothers Grimm's version of this European fairy tale, so Caperucita was part of the collective folk memory of Argentina long before the comedian invented Caperuciten. This is demonstrated by the monument, which is surely one of the most delightful ever to have been dedicated to the little girl with the distinctive red headgear. It was acquired in 1937 by the city government of Buenos Aires and originally stood on Plaza Lavalle, not far from Avenida Córdoba. When a statue of ex-president Hipólito Yrigoyen was erected on that spot in 1972, Caperucita was taken to a new site that actually seems much more fitting than the old one: she was placed in the "woods of Palermo," an extensive park on the north side of the city center.

The French artist Jean Carlus (1852–1930) sculpted Red Riding Hood from a single block of marble. The wolf is peering cunningly from behind a tree trunk and attempting to lure the girl, who is holding a picnic basket in one hand and a bunch of flowers in the other, into its trap.

Address Parque Tres de Febrero, corner of Av. Sarmiento and Av. Libertador, Palermo, CABA | **Getting there** Subte D to Plaza Italia, then walk seven *cuadras* along Av. Sarmiento or take bus 10, 37, or 67 | **Tip** The Museo Evita is within walking distance (Lafinur 2988, Tue–Sun 11am–7pm).

86_Regazzoni's Studio

The eccentric railway artist

Since Carlos Regazzoni took over these three sheds at Retiro station in the 1980s, railways have been the theme at the heart of his extraordinary works. For some years, he created monstrous insects from railway scrap, and in paintings, too, he puts locomotives and tracks on canvas in all sorts of crazy ways. In the egocentric manner of Salvador Dalí, Regazzoni sees himself as a great artist, using the waste of the Industrial Revolution to produce works that transform society.

And though Regazzoni may be far from achieving the global fame of Salvador Dalí, the works of this sculptor with a head of wild, matted gray hair are nevertheless impressive. He made his breakthrough in the alternative art scene in 1991, when the French filmmaker Franck Joseph presented an account of him. He traveled to Paris several times and had exhibitions more frequently in Argentina from that time. One of his paintings was shown at MALBA in Buenos Aires.

At first sight, his studio is not an inviting place. When you first set foot on the site, you might think you are in a scrapyard. It takes a little while for the art to emerge, between puddles and old bits of iron and steel. In the "habitat of the old cat," as he calls his realm, Regazzoni works, thinks, eats, and holds parties. He sleeps in an old carriage. He also runs a restaurant that serves "railway meals." His specialty is wild boar in red-wine sauce. Every weekend he organizes a performance of live music there, and a wine-tasting evening in this railway world with industrial surroundings is an unforgettable experience for anyone who is staying in Buenos Aires.

The studio is also open during the day for anyone at any time, however. Not only that: any newcomer can exhibit his or her paintings here without asking for permission. Regazzoni may be a little too pleased with himself at times, but he does live by some good principles.

Address Av. del Libertador, near Suipacha, Retiro, CABA | **Getting there** Mitre, Belgrano Norte, and San Martín lines, or Subte C to Retiro, then walk along Av. Libertador parallel to the tracks as far as the first turning (entrance to the left of the Museo Nacional Ferroviario); bus 17, 61, 62, 67, 92, 93, 110, 124, or 130 | **Hours** Pub with live music every Thu & Fri from 9pm | **Tip** To complement this, visit the Museo Nacional Ferroviario with its old carriages, steam locomotives, and antique railway paraphernalia (Av. del Libertador 405, Mon–Fri 9:30am–5pm, Sat & Sun 10:30am–6pm, closed on holidays).

87 Reserva Costanera Norte

A neglected artificial river oasis

In the 1960s, to make space for a new university campus, land was reclaimed on the banks of the Río de la Plata. In the course of the works, this peninsula with an area of some 18 hectares was created near Nuñez – and was not built up.

Over the years, nature reclaimed the site, as seeds were washed up by the river. Willow and alder trees put down roots, several species of birds colonized the land, and a lagoon with turtles was established. An entirely neglected natural river oasis formed on an artificially created site. The only human residents were a group of homosexuals who lived here in the 1980s, looking for a refuge from marginalization and violence. The informal settlement known as Villa Gay was later taken over by homeless families, who were evicted in 2006, when a natural park was planned here as part of a large construction project.

The excavators moved in almost secretly and began to lay big concrete slabs on the peninsula. By the time environmentalists discovered the building site, much of the woodland had already given way to concrete. Thanks to pressure from public opinion, construction stopped and the land was given protection as a nature reserve. Regulations passed in 2012 laid down measures to preserve the Reserva Costanera Norte, but nothing has happened since then, as the city government and the university, which owns the site, were unable to agree, even though there is an urgent need to ensure that the lagoon does not dry out and that no further illegal hunting of birds takes place.

Until the responsible authorities do their job, committed citizens are trying to bring life to the nature reserve, organizing readings and musical walks through the beautiful, peaceful woods. It is fascinating to observe how nature asserts itself against concrete. Grass and shrubs are emerging between the slabs – it really is a forgotten oasis!

Address The shore behind Ciudad Universitaria, Nuñez, CABA | **Getting there** Belgrano Norte train line from Retiro to Ciudad Universitaria, then walk to the university; bus 28, 33, 37, 42, 45, 107, or 160, access behind the south-eastern faculty building, passing to the left of the sewage plant | **Hours** Unrestricted, but best avoided at night; for events, see the Facebook page of the Amigos de Costanera Norte | **Tip** You can combine a visit to the nature reserve with a walk around the Velatropa ecological village (see ch. 110).

88 The Retiro Stations

The three musketeers of suburban transport

If you ask for directions to the main station in Buenos Aires, you might get as many as six different answers. Depending on which direction you want to take in the metropolitan area, there is a train line to match, each with its own station. Alongside Constitución, Once, and Lacroze, Retiro is the main transport hub of the city. Three train stations stand here, one next to the other.

The oldest and largest of them is at the corner of Avenida Libertador, on the site of the Estación Central, which burned down in 1897. A new station had to be built, and so Mitre was opened in 1915. It was designed in the style of 19th-century European stations, with a huge concourse, ornate ticket desks and Florentine torches. Like the other stations, it was designed by a firm of British architects and British engineer Reginald Reynolds.

The station at the center is Belgrano, built in 1912 in a French style. Next to it stands a rickety-looking wooden structure dating from 1930. San Martín is the last of the three stations to be built, and was only intended to be temporary. The stone building that was supposed to replace it was never constructed. Together, these three stations make up Retiro. They differ not only in their architectural style: the trains depart and arrive on tracks with three different gauges.

It used to be possible to catch a train from here to the northern provinces of Argentina. However, most of these connections fell victim to a ping-pong game of alternating privatization and nationalization. For President Perón, the rail network was a symbol of independence from Britain. He therefore nationalized it in the period after 1946. This was followed by reprivatization in the 1990s under President Menem, and then part-nationalization in the Kirchner years. One feature from the network's British roots has survived all of this: to this day, all trains drive on the left.

Address Av. Ramos Mejía, Retiro, CABA | **Getting there** Mitre, Belgrano Norte, or San Martín line, or Subte C to Retiro; bus 5, 6, 7, 9, 20, 22, 23, 26, 28, 33, and others | **Hours** Trains run between 5am and 11pm; watch out for pickpockets, especially after dark | **Tip** On Plaza San Martín, above Av. Libertador, stands a monument with an eternal flame for those who fell in the Falklands/Malvinas War.

89_The Roca Monument

A controversial statue to a murderer

It is a game of cat and mouse: as soon as the authorities have removed the graffiti saying "genocide" and "murderer" from the plinth of the statue, someone renews them.

No historical figure is as controversial in Argentina as General Julio Argentino Roca (1843–1914). The bronze monument that has honored him since 1941 on one of the city's main traffic arteries is the focus of a dispute about how the origin of the Argentinian state should be interpreted.

After independence, different rulers waged war on the indigenous population with the aim of gaining their territories. From 1878, Roca was minister of war, responsible for the final phase of the systematic conquest of Patagonia and the pampas. He made an unequivocal statement about his mission to a newspaper: "Let us therefore destroy this people with a clear conscience, annihilate their resources and political organization so that their tribal structure disappears and if necessary their families are dissolved."

To this day, many Argentinians believe that the "barbarian" indigenous peoples had to be fought in the interests of civilization. Human-rights activists vehemently reject this and criticize the fact that the "conquest of the desert," as the campaigns were called, is still depicted on the reverse side of the 100-peso note. They demand the removal of Roca's monument. Those who defend the equestrian statue, by contrast, call for appreciation of Roca's later achievements as president. Among other measures, he introduced free schooling. His supporters claim that anyone who wants to take down the monument should also argue for the abolition of free school education. In some provinces, streets named for Roca have been renamed Néstor Kirchner Street. This, in turn, mobilized opponents of ex-president Kirchner, who died in 2010. The debate about Roca will not be over anytime soon.

Address Crossroads of Av. Presidente Julio A. Roca (Diagonal Sur) and Adolfo Alsina, Monserrat, CABA | **Getting there** Subte E to Bolívar, Subte A to Perú, Subte D to Catedral; bus 2, 8, 22, 24, 28, 29, 56, 64, 86, 91, and others | **Tip** Next to the statue is Manzana de las Luces, with the Jesuits' underground tunnels (see ch. 52).

90 The Ruined Vasena Factory

Silent testimony to a bloody labor dispute

Nothing would serve as a reminder of the bloodbath that was perpetrated here were it not for two walls at the very edge of Plaza Martín Fierro. They are the neglected remains of a factory owned by the Italian Vasena family, who were major metal producers in the early 20th century. On January 7, 1919 their workers went on strike, demanding better conditions of work. Within just one week there was an escalation of violence that went down in the history books as the Semana Trágica.

Following the Bolshevik Revolution in Russia in 1917, the elites on the Río de la Plata were gripped by fears that Russian-born Jews would bring the spirit of revolution from Europe to Argentina. When the Vasena strike began, it was thought to be the start of a workers' revolution. For several days, the police and ultra-right groups joined together to shoot at the strikers. In fury, the militant workers burned down the Vasena factory. The consequence of this was that strikers were hunted down. The districts where they lived, union offices, and Jewish institutions were attacked. The workers ended the strike only when President Yrigoyen came to an agreement with the trade unions. At the conclusion of the "tragic week," 1,300 people were dead and 5,000 injured.

Depending on the political leanings of the governments of the following years, blame for this violence was laid either at the feet of the workers, condemned as terrorists, or the police and the government of the time. When the plaza was inaugurated in 1940 on the site of the ruined factory, conservatives were in power and it was not named for the "martyrs of Semana Trágica," as some demanded, but after the hero of the Argentinian national epic poem, Martín Fierro. A plaque on the remains of the factory commemorates these awful events and the beginning of a long period of workers' struggles.

Address Plaza Martín Fierro, between La Rioja and Gral, Urquiza, San Cristóbal, CABA | **Getting there** Subte E to Urquiza; bus 31, 53, 97, 101, 126, or 129A | **Tip** At the crossing of Av. San Juan and Av. Boedo, four *cuadras* from the Urquiza Subte stop, are several traditional tango bars, for example La Esquina (dinner with tango show daily at 10pm, booking advisable).

91_The Russian Orthodox Church

Blue onion domes above Parque Lezama

The ornate blue onion domes rise splendidly into the sky above San Telmo. There is probably no building in the city that is architecturally and stylistically so distinctive as the Russian Orthodox Church of the Holy Trinity next to Parque Lezama. Built in the style of cruciform, domed Russian churches of the 17th century, it is the focal point of Russian Orthodox life in Buenos Aires. The designs were conceived in Saint Petersburg and later adapted in Buenos Aires. After four years of construction, it was consecrated in 1901 in the presence of international representatives of the Orthodox church and President Julio A. Roca.

The opulent interior decoration comes from Russia and is strictly arranged according to the rules of the Orthodox Church. The altar is at the east end and there is no organ, as God may be praised here by the human voice alone. The highlights are the magnificently gilded chancel, the colorful stained-glass windows, and the large mural painting that extends across the whole width of the interior. The crosses on the roof are attached to the onion domes with golden chains, and also point east. No one who has seen the church from inside will be surprised to learn that it has been declared a national historic monument.

This was the first Russian Orthodox church on the whole South American continent. The first Orthodox Christians came to the Río de la Plata in the mid-19th century, mostly from Russia and Greece, but there was nowhere for them to worship. In 1888, the Russian tsar therefore decreed that this congregation should be founded. To this day, the bishop who has his see here is responsible for the whole of South America and subordinate to the patriarch of Moscow. Today the population of Russians and people of Russian origin in Argentina numbers up to 300,000, more than anywhere else in South America.

Address Avenida Brasil 315, San Telmo, CABA | **Getting there** Subte C to Constitución; bus 4, 10, 22, 24, 28, 29, 46, 53, 61, 62, and others | **Hours** Guests are welcome at church services; for guided tours call +11/4361427 or info@iglesiarusa.org.ar, usually on the 2nd Sunday in the month at 3pm, by arrangement in English. Women are asked to wear a skirt and cover their heads, men should wear long trousers. | **Tip** In Parque Lezama an elegant mansion dating from 1891 houses the National Historical Museum (Defensa 1600, Wed–Sun 11am–6pm).

92 Sabato's House

The private rooms of a great artist

While Sabato, holder of the Cervantes Prize, was still alive, insiders knew about the enchantment of his house, where he wrote all of his books. In 1945 his family bought it from a cinema pioneer who had built it in 1927, without architectural knowledge but with great creativity. Fans often tried to glimpse Sabato over the fence. Now, after his death, the interior of the Casa de Ernesto Sabato is open to visitors.

Sabato accompanied Argentina through the 20th century, before dying here on April 30, 2011, shortly before his 100th birthday. A physicist, in 1945 he gave up science and devoted himself exclusively to writing. He became known internationally in 1948 with the novel *El Túnel*. At the request of President Alfonsín he chaired the commission on the crimes of the last military junta in Argentina. Its world-famous report *Nunca más* (Never Again) was drawn up under his direction. In the years up to his death, Sabato expressed himself on political issues again and again.

In his house, the artist himself now guides visitors through the library, study, and atelier. How is that possible? His son Mario, a filmmaker by profession, recorded his father over a period of years. Short sequences in every room provide insights into the charming nature of this literary figure. Sabato personally explains his obsession with orderliness, which is maintained here with extreme care: every single one of the 7,000 books stands exactly in the place where he put it.

It is important to his descendants to keep everything as it was in Sabato's lifetime. They renovated the house themselves and opened it in 2014 as a living museum. His grandchildren are the tour guides.

They are especially proud of Ernesto's legacy as a painter. His pictures were exhibited only twice. One of those occasions was in the famous Centre Pompidou in Paris. Exactly the same works are now shown in the studio.

Address Saverio Langeri 3135, Santos Lugares, Provincia | **Getting there** San Martín train from Retiro to Santos Lugares; bus 105 | **Hours** Sat 1–5pm, free tours given by his grandchildren every hour; see the Facebook page for the latest information | **Tip** If you are in this part of the city, round off the day in Café de García (see ch. 16), two stops from Santos Lugares by train in the direction of Retiro (Devoto).

93 The Secret

When marble comes alive

Little Eros stretches up to his mother Aphrodite on tiptoe. Over her knee, a cloth is spread lightly. She bends down carefully, smiles, and looks attentively to one side as Eros whispers a secret in her ear. The vivacity that the German artist Gustav Eberlein (1847–1926) breathed into his sculpture *El Secreto* is most impressive. You can positively hear the electric crackle of the secret that is being revealed here.

Eberlein made this group in 1891 from precious Carrara marble. Today, it stands in the Galería de los Bustos, a foyer of the Teatro Colón, beneath the busts of famous composers. Nothing is left to chance here, in the leading opera house of Latin America. It is rumored that these Greek deities of love were placed here to delight the hearts of opera goers who take their drinks in the foyer and philosophize about music. More than one couple is said to have been brought together as a result of the striking aura of this marble sculpture with a living soul.

Presumably they speculated, as they flirted, on what Eros might be whispering to Aphrodite. Perhaps a few secrets about regular visitors to the opera? Or secrets about the Teatro Colón itself? For example, the fact that until 1888 it stood on Plaza de Mayo and served all year round as an ice store for the restaurants of the city, with more than 1,000 tonnes of ice in its cellar. Or that the main entrance of the new building is situated on Plaza Lavalle rather than on the showcase boulevard 9 de Julio, which did not yet exist when the theater was opened in 1908. And that in 2006 it was closed for four years for renovation work, and for lack of funds could not be reopened as planned to celebrate the hundredth anniversary of the opera house itself – the reopening only took place to commemorate 200 years of national independence. Oh yes – it would be interesting to hear the details of Eros' secret.

Address Teatro Colón, Tucumán 1171, San Nicolás, CABA | Getting there Subte B to Carlos Pellegrini, Subte C to Lavalle, Subte D to Tribunales; bus 5, 7, 9, 10, 17, 23, 29, 39, 45, 59, and others | Hours Tours daily 9am–5pm, every 15 minutes (except May 1, Dec 24/25/31, & Jan 1, and during performances) | Tip Mirador Massue at the corner of Tucumán and Talcahuano is a 20th-century building. In 1989, much of it was rebuilt and glazed. Only the corner tower is original, a contrast to the modern rebuilding.

94 Seat of the Society of Madres de la Plaza de Mayo

A rendezvous for political debate

On the walls of the Café Revolucionario hang pictures of more or less every revolutionary in recent history. For each of them, a red star shines on a large memorial plaque. Most people only know this place as a nice café with the Che Guevara look where you can eat well at a reasonable price. But there is more to it. Passing through the café, you reach the offices and meeting rooms of the Asociación Madres de la Plaza de Mayo. The association of the Mothers of the Square of the May Revolution is a human-rights organization, founded by Argentinian women whose children and grandchildren were abducted and murdered by the armed forces during the dictatorship between 1976 and 1983. They demanded the release of their children and information on their whereabouts. Later they devoted themselves to prosecution of these crimes in the law courts and to preserving the memory of what happened in Argentina. To this day, mothers and fathers are looking for their children who were taken away by force in those years (see ch. 24).

Until 2017 the rooms behind the Café Revolucionario included the specially founded people's university of the Madres. In 2000, they began to promote critical thinking by means of several short courses of study connected with human rights. Whereas they received generous support from the left-wing Kirchner government, under the neoliberal Macri, who came to power in 2015, the university was forced to close down. Its reputation had suffered considerably at the end due to accusations of corruption. In the politically heated and polarized situation of conflict in the country, it is difficult to assess who is telling the truth. It is worth forming your own opinion by visiting the seat of the association, close to the Congress building – not only the remarkable atmosphere of the café, but also the bookshop and events program of the Madres provide insights into the recent political history of Argentina.

Address Hipólito Yrigoyen 1584, Monserrat, CABA | **Getting there** Subte A to Sáenz Peña; bus 8, 23, 39, 56, 60, 64, 86, 102, 105, 151, or 168 | **Hours** Café Mon–Sat 8am–midnight | **Tip** On the corner of Av. Callao and Av. Rivadavia is the Art Nouveau building of a once legendary coffee house, El Molino. Note the windmill sails on its tower.

95_The Signs of Memory

Analysing history in pictograms

When the artists of the Grupo de Arte Callejero began to work on their Signs of Memory, most of the men guilty of repression in General Videla's military regime were walking around free. President Carlos Menem had ensured this by means of various amnesty laws in the 1990s. Inspired by the realization that the people responsible for state terror were living among them, the artists had the idea of creating this remarkable installation, part of the Parque de la Memoria commemorative site, which was opened in 2001.

More than 50 traffic signs, artistically remodeled, lead visitors through recent Argentinian history along the waterside promenade. They are devoted to the violent rules of the military dictatorship and refer to the antecedents and consequences of the atrocities that were committed.

Using the codes of traffic signs that everybody knows, the artists succeeded in an intriguing way in revealing the causes, effects, and results of dictatorship and linking them together – from the Alianza Anticomunista Argentina, the ultra-right paramilitary group from which the army adopted its methods and aims, to the flight into exile of thousands of citizens, the murders, and the role of civilian organizations. Some of the signs are also dedicated to the circumstances of world history and in Latin America that made the rise of the military government possible. At the center of the 14-hectare Parque de la Memoria stands a long stone wall, onto which the names of 30,000 victims of the dictatorship have been inscribed. The closeness of the site to the Río de la Plata has important symbolic meaning: many of the people who "disappeared" were thrown into the river from planes. Some bodies were found later, but many were carried out into the open sea. The message of these traffic signs is unambiguous: may these crimes never again be committed!

Address Av. Costanera Rafael Obligado 6745, Belgrano, CABA | **Getting there** Belgrano Norte train line from Retiro to Ciudad Universitaria, then walk through the campus to the river bank, or bus 28, 33, 37, 42, 45, 107, or 160 to the park entrance | **Hours** Mon–Fri 10am–6pm, Sat, Sun, & holidays 10am–7pm; for guided tours, inquire at www.parquedelamemoria.org.ar | **Tip** PayS (Presentes, Ahora y Siempre) on this site is an art center on the subject of state terrorism, where exhibitions and conferences are held (Mon–Fri 10am–5pm, Sat, Sun, & holidays 11am–6pm).

96 Simik Photography Café

Truly a museum café

Café Palacios is cozy and inexpensive, and has a small but high-quality choice of quickly prepared meals. So far, so boring. This description can be applied to hundreds of cafés in Buenos Aires and for 40 years would have been perfectly adequate to denote the character of this eatery on a corner close to Chacarita cemetery. However, its proprietor, Alejandro Simik, was in search of some occupation during the economic crisis of 2002 – in order to avoid having to visit a psychologist, as he himself said. He began to collect cameras, and transformed his café into an exhibition space. Since then it has turned into an exceptional gem of the local gastronomic scene – or, should we say, the museum scene?

The museum and café blend into one another. Beneath the glass tops of the tables lie miniature collections of items from a particular era or examples of a specific kind of accessory, such as rolls of film, flash attachments, or cleaning utensils. In the large showcases that act as partitions, some 2,000 cameras trace the historical development of photography. They include folding-bellows models, the oldest of which dates back to 1870. On the first Wednesday in every month a new photographic exhibition is opened. As a result, the small Café Palacios is crammed from floor to ceiling with works of art and exhibits, but this constitutes its special charm.

The café museum long ago became a focal point of the local photographic scene. Amateur and professional photographers can often be seen with their digital and analog cameras, drinking a cup of coffee or a glass of wine together, chatting about new models and old dark-room techniques.

Simik organizes talks and has a black-and-white laboratory in his cellar that is open to everyone. On Tuesdays from 8pm a jazz band plays – a second passion of Alejandro Simik that he wanted to make part of his café.

Address Av. Federico Lacroze 3901, Chacarita, CABA | Getting there Subte B to Lacroze; bus 19, 39, 42, 44, 47, 63, 65, 71, 76, 87, and others | Hours Mon–Sat 8am–midnight. The museum also runs low-cost photography courses at beginner's and advanced level. If you have a long stay in Buenos Aires, go to the café or Facebook for information. | Tip Between Lacroze station and Simik café on Av. Lacroze are some down-to-earth grill restaurants serving excellent meat and delicious sausages with no frills.

97 The Stadiums of Racing and Independiente

El Clásico de Avellaneda

"To whom do you belong?" This question is often asked in Buenos Aires. It relates to football clubs. Nowhere in the world are there so many first-division clubs in such a small area as in Buenos Aires. In Avellaneda two arch-rivals even play cheek by jowl. The stadiums of Atlético Independiente and Racing are no more than 300 meters apart. This closeness constantly fuels the historic sporting rivalry between the two clubs. Since the early 20th century this competitive spirit has been maintained at least as intensely as that between the famous clubs Boca Juniors and River Plate. The home ground of Independiente is called Libertadores de América. It is a rectangular stadium that holds 50,000 spectators. The arena where Racing play is called Presidente Perón, but its circular shape has given it the nickname El Coliseo. It originally accommodated 100,000 spectators, but renovation and regulations reduced the capacity to 51,000.

When the two teams play a home game at the same time, in one stadium you can hear the chanting of the fans coming from the other. From the top tiers in the stands of Libertadores de América you can even see the roof of the Racing stadium across the way. And when the two rivals play each other in a derby, in the so-called Clásico de Avellaneda, the players change and warm up in their own ground before taking a relaxed stroll to their opponents' stadium shortly before the match kicks off. In the historical statistics of encounters between the two, Independiente has come out as the clear leader.

Fans only ever get to see the inside of the opponents' stadium on television: since 2013 admission to the ground has been prohibited to away supporters in Argentina. The violence of the Barra Bravas, the local ultras, had gone too far, and fatal shootings had repeatedly taken place.

Address Between Av. Adolfo Alsina, Colón, Italia, and Ricardo Enrique Bochini, Avellaneda, Provincia | Getting there Roca train line from Constitución, all go to Avellaneda; bus 10, 98, 100, 134, or 148 | Hours Visits when no game is taking place aren't possible at the moment | Tip At the corner of Italia and Av. Belgrano stands the impressive Hospital Fiorito, dating from 1913, one of the main health institutions in the south of the Buenos Aires metropolitan area.

98 Station Pasteur

Memories of the AMIA bombing in July 1994

Between the columns of Pasteur subway station hangs a large clock with fold-over digits. Its minute display does move, but always to the same time. The clock is mourning a tragic moment in the history of the city: on July 18, 1994, at exactly 9:53am, a 400-kilogram bomb exploded in front of the building of the Asociación Mutual Israelita Argentina (AMIA), the leading Jewish center in Buenos Aires. There were 85 fatalities and 300 were injured, making this the worst terrorist attack in the history of Argentina. In 2007, charges were brought against the alleged planners of the attack, members of Hizbollah and representatives of the Iranian government, but to this day nobody has been sentenced.

In January 2015, Alberto Nisman, the special state prosecutor, accused President Cristina Kirchner of having actively prevented prosecution of the suspects with the aim of protecting the Iranian planners of the bombing from punishment – hoping to conclude an attractive business agreement for Argentina in return. Nisman also accused Carlos Menem of blocking the investigations during his period in office. The family of the ex-president, who come from Syria, are said to have had links to one of the main suspects. A few hours before Nisman was due to present his accusation to parliament, he was found dead in his flat. He had been shot. In late 2017, a court of law concluded that it was murder and not, as was long asserted, suicide.

Station Pasteur has become a place for artistic commemoration. Humorous drawings on the walls by 24 artists are concerned with the bombing and the snail's-pace investigation. An addition has been made to the name of the Subte station: it is now called Pasteur – Amia. The clock will display the same time of day until the people responsible have been sentenced. AMIA is only two *cuadras* from the station. Its new building is shielded by a high wall.

Address Station entrance Av. Corrientes (near no. 3200), corner of Pasteur and Balvanera, CABA | **Getting there** Subte B to Pasteur – Amia | **Hours** Mon–Sat 6am–10pm, Sun 8am–10pm | **Tip** A model of the destroyed AMIA building that was made for the investigations is in the police museum (see ch. 36).

99_The Statue of Liberty

Much smaller. And what about the liberty?

The Statue of Liberty in New York may well be the world's most-copied statue. In the USA alone there are said to be more than 50 copies of this representation of the Roman goddess Libertas. You can also find versions in Tokyo, Paris, and even Cuba. But this one, hidden between trees at the edge of the Plaza Barrancas de Belgrano, truly shares the genes of its sister, the famous original statue on Liberty Island in New York.

It was created by the same French artist, Frédéric-Auguste Bartholdi, and inaugurated on October 3, 1886, 25 days before the one in New York. So this is the older version, though at 4 meters only a bonsai version of the 46-meter monument off Manhattan. The two statues are also different colors. Whereas the large one watches over the Hudson River wearing a turquoise robe, owing to oxidation of the copper, the small one on the Río de la Plata is black, as it was made from iron.

If you would like to test its authenticity, you have to take a close look: the sculptor's signature is inscribed on the base, and the words "Fondu par Le Val D'Osne 68, 8 rue Voltaire, Paris" refer to the forge whose products were so popular in the 19th century that many cities ordered a statue to be cast there. Only the USA was presented with one as a gift from the French people on the occasion of the 100th anniversary of independence.

Perhaps its diminutive size is the reason why *Libertas porteña* is not especially well known. You can test this by asking people about the Estatua de la Libertad. Not many have ever heard of it. And if they do know it, then usually they add a derisive comment. For example, that Argentina is much less free than the USA, which matches the size of the statue. And photos show that for many years a graffiti slogan could be read at its foot: "La libertad no es estatua. Ella vuela." – "Freedom is no statue. It flies."

Address Plaza Barrancas de Belgrano, La Pampa between Virrey Vértiz and Arribeños, Belgrano, CABA | Getting there Subte D to José Hernández or Juramento, or the Mitre train from Retiro to Belgrano C; bus 15, 29, 42, 55, 60, 64, 118, or 130 | Tip The northern end of the plaza, right next to Station Belgrano C, is the start of the Barrio Chino (Chinatown), where you can see something else that Buenos Aires and New York have in common.

100 Street Art in Coghlan and Villa Urquiza

Subversively legal

Buenos Aires is heaven for practitioners of street art. Spraying is legal, provided you ask the owner of the building for permission. As the movement is still relatively new locally and the city is big, many spaces are still available. By the early 1980s, lively street-art scenes were already established in the USA and Europe. In Buenos Aires this was out of the question during the years of military dictatorship. It was not until the 1990s that the first street artists started to paint the walls here. Today Buenos Aires is regarded as one of the leading cities in South America for street art. Sprayed paintings are everywhere, but to see the most impressive and memorable works, you have to travel out to the margins of the city.

The oldest murals are to be found in Villa Urquiza, for example a work by the anonymous Italian artist Blu (Holmberg 2705). It depicts a man with an outsized head lying down. The colors have already faded and the owners of the house recently gave the work a surround in pale grey. The artist was not pleased at all. It is possible that he will now paint over the mural completely, as he did in 2014 to his Cuvry graffiti in Berlin in protest against the gentrification of the area.

The Coghlan district was taken by storm by street artists during the course of 2014. Several owners were delighted, and now pay to have their house walls painted. But in Buenos Aires, as elsewhere, street art often has a political motivation: at Naón 3300 a military tortoise pulls a little cart with children playing in an intact bubble. This is a joint work by the Argentinian-Australian duo Martin Ron and Fintan Magee.

Street art is fast-moving! Matt from BA Street Art is always up to date, and his guided tours are highly recommended.

Address Tour starts at Drago station, follows Holmberg, then the corner of Av. Congreso and Tronador, continuing east on Av. Congreso, then north on Estomba as far as Nuñez, CABA | **Getting there** Mitre train line from Retiro toward Suárez to Drago or Coghlan; bus 107, 114, 169, or 175 | **Hours** Tours with BA Street Art Tue, Thu & Sat 2:45pm, information and booking at www.buenosairesstreetart.com | **Tip** The best beer in town is close by at the brew-pub Cervecería Bar Spangher (Miller 2901, from 7pm), with three kinds made on site; Cervecería Cossab (Ignacio Rivera 4700, from 7pm) serves a wide range of national cervezas artesanales and international beers.

101 The Street of Cinemas

Tombstone for a picture palace

The life cycle of Lavalle in the Microcentro has turned around 180 degrees. In the daytime it is a bustling shopping street where stores selling trash and souvenirs alternate with expensive tourist restaurants. It used to be called Calle de los Cines, the street of cinemas, and was one of the most popular nightlife spots in Buenos Aires. As many as 52,000 people flocked to its five *cuadras* in the evenings. Today, Lavalle is almost deserted after dark. Only the red lights of the bingo halls shine onto the gray paving. Almost nothing remains of the former glory of 20 cinemas.

If you take a walk, keeping your eyes open, you will see marble plaques set into the ground on the left and right along Lavalle. They are silent witnesses to the old days. Engraved letters such as "Luxor: 1920–1993" are hardly distinguishable now, after countless feet have trodden them without noticing. But these stones are memorials to the cinemas that once stood here.

In the Golden Twenties, when the first picture palaces appeared in Lavalle, silent movies were accompanied by live orchestras and tango singers. More and more, larger and larger cinemas were built. In the 1950s the big fast-food restaurants joined them. In the 1990s, when shopping malls with multi-screen cinemas came to Buenos Aires, the old picture houses in Lavalle were uncompetitive. They gave way to restaurants and retail spaces, and a Pentecostal church for charismatic Christianity even converted a film auditorium into a space for preaching.

In spite of financial crises and internet streaming services, the enthusiasm for cinemas has remained alive in Buenos Aires. More than 200 movie halls still exist to bear witness to this, including many old-established and alternate arthouse cinemas. And what could better express a deep love of the silver screen than tombstones for those who have passed away?

Address Lavalle (west of the crossing with Florida), San Nicolás, CABA | **Getting there** Subte B to Florida, Subte C to Lavalle; bus 6, 22, 23, 26, 28, 33, 45, 50, 56, 61, and others | **Tip** To get an impression of how splendid Lavalle must once have been, take a night-time walk along the parallel street Av. Corrientes, today home to theater, musicals, and ballet shows.

102 Taller Clandestino

"These clothes smell of death"

You could see this tragedy coming: on April 27, 2015 two brothers aged seven and ten died when their sweatshop in the district of Flores went up in flames. Flores has a concentration of illegal textile workshops.

In conditions similar to slavery, around 30,000 people in and around Buenos Aires produce clothes for the national and international market. Often, they are underage workers whose passports have been taken from them. They sleep in the rooms in which they have to labor at sewing machines for up to 14 hours a day for 60 cents per hour. The ventilation is usually poor, and fatal accidents are not uncommon in these so-called *talleres clandestinos*.

In the burnt-out ruin at Páez 2796, scorched bales of fabric were still lying untouched in the burnt-out rooms months after the fire. There was no sign that anyone would come to clear up.

"End slave labor" and "these clothes smell of death" is written on the walls of the building. The doors and windows had been bricked up to conceal what was happening behind the walls – walls that blocked the boys' escape route from the blazing sweatshop.

Three months later, only a few minutes' walk from here, a mural was painted in memory of the two victims. Street artists draped two boys in scraps of cloth that they had collected in the illegal workshop.

Some 80 percent of clothes in Argentina are made illegally. Most of them end up in La Salada, the biggest tolerated black market in Latin America, which is in Buenos Aires Provincia. It has a turnover of about $9 million per week and gives employment to approximately 6,000 people. All of this is well known, but nothing happens to stop it – although, according to Argentinian law, companies are responsible for the entire production chain. The 100 or so international fashion retailers whose clothing is produced here could easily be held to account for the conditions of manufacture.

Address Ruin: Páez 2796, Flores, CABA. Mural: corner of Gavilán and Méndez de Andes, Flores, CABA | **Getting there** Ruin: Subte A to San Pedrito; bus 53, 63, 84, 106, 124, 133, 134, or 181. Mural: Subte A to San José de Flores; bus 92, 99, 113, 124, or 172. | **Tip** From the mural it is only five *cuadras* to part of Korea Town and the Korean monument on Plaza Angel Gris (see ch. 9).

103 Teatro Catalinas Sur

By neighbors for neighbors

The Catalinas Sur ensemble is a drama group that plays in and for the district of La Boca, as you can tell from a glance at the façade of their modest theater shack. A mural depicts the great steel bridge, the emblem of the *barrio*, along with dock workers and a bandoneon player. Although this theater group is now renowned far beyond La Boca, and many of the 300 amateur actors come from other parts of the city, it remains true to its original principle: "theater by neighbors for neighbors."

Catalinas Sur are the pioneers of *teatro comunitario* in Argentina. This movement started up in the 1980s with the aim of strengthening communal solidarity in the *barrios* with the help of theater. Following a decade when mistrust and fear were sown by the military regime, this neighborhood theater became a place for encounter and dialog. Starting from a conviction that every person is a source of creativity, the idea was that the act of neighbors making theater together would contribute to a change in society.

It all began with a play that they performed on a public plaza in 1984. A small group of people from the Catalinas Sur area had produced it themselves, and they performed it unannounced – they called it a "theatrical party." So soon after the restoration of democracy, no one had yet dared to do such a thing.

A great deal has happened since then. Catalinas Sur have their own house, and have been on tour in Argentina and Spain. Today there are about 59 groups like this in Argentina, and a national network of *teatros comunitarios* exists. The Catalinas Sur ensemble is well established in the alternative theater scene of Buenos Aires. Its plays are about the lives and dreams of residents of La Boca. If you can speak Spanish, do not fail to see one of their performances. Apart from that, the theater building with its numerous figures is definitely worth seeing.

Address B. Pérez Galdós 93, La Boca, CABA | Getting there Bus 20, 25, 29, 33, 53, 54, 64, 86, 129M, 130, 152, 159, or 186 | Note In the La Boca district, poverty and lack of prospects have led to an increased crime rate. If you don't know your way around, don't explore this area on foot. You can get to the theater by taxi and bus without problems. | Hours Box office: Tue–Sat 3–9pm, +11/43005707 | Tip Round the corner, Usina del Arte (Pedro de Mendoza/Pérez Galdós) is a former electricity works dating from 1916 that has been converted into a municipal arts center.

104_Teatro Verdi

Classics, football, and class struggle

Every stone of the Teatro Verdi breathes history. Built in 1901 by the Sociedad de Socorros Mutuos José Verdi for the promotion of "vocal and instrumental music," it quickly became much more than a musical institution in the La Boca port quarter. Numerous plaques in the lobby serve as reminders of political and social achievements that originated here.

The boxes, which are painted in the original colors of the association – turquoise, white, and gold – were occupied not only by audiences for classical concerts. In 1903, Alfredo Palacios, who was put forward as candidate for La Boca in the elections for the house of representatives, was acclaimed here by his supporters. The following year he was elected, the first socialist deputy in the Americas. Later, the Argentinian Communist Party was founded in the Teatro Verdi.

The stage with its boards of solid pine, a little worn today but still imposing, was not only used by the great tango singers. Here the board of the football club Boca Juniors announced its intention to build a new stadium – La Bonbonera, opened in 1940 and still one of the world's best-known arenas. Boca Juniors' arch-rivals from the River Plate club also held their first general meetings in the Teatro Verdi. In the 1970s and 1980s the leading national rock musicians, for example the cult band Sumo (see ch. 63), also performed on this historic stage.

The façade outside is adorned by a bust of the Italian composer Guiseppe Verdi, who gave the theater and the society their name. The first work that the house orchestra played here was an opera by Verdi. At this, the decision was taken to dedicate the theater to him, while translating his first name into Spanish – José. Shortly before his death in 1901, Verdi expressed his thanks in writing for this honor. The hand-written letter is carefully preserved in the society's office next to the theater.

Address Av. Almirante Brown 736, La Boca, CABA | **Getting there** Bus 20, 25, 29, 33, 53, 64, 86, 129LM, 130, 152, or 159 | **Hours** First Sat of the month, folklore, and first Wed of the month, tango from 8pm; information on other events: Jckehiayan@yahoo.com.ar or +11/43621321, Mon–Fri 2–7pm. At these times the office to the left of the theater (no. 719) is open. The friendly people who run the theater will be pleased to show its interior to anyone in possession of this book. | **Tip** Walk toward the docks to enjoy excellent meat in the restaurant El Obrero with the most authentic harbor atmosphere in La Boca (Agustín R. Caffarena 64, Mon–Sat noon–4pm and from 8pm), a real tip for insiders that came within a whisker of getting a page to itself in this book! For safety reasons, arrive by taxi.

105_Tierra Santa

Disneyland for Christians

On the Costanera, beneath the flight path for the airport, which is only a few minutes' walk away, there lies in the shadow of the high-rises of Palermo a scene that, it has to be admitted, is a little bit strange.

Tierra Santa is a leisure park that tells the story of the New Testament. At its heart is the hill of Golgotha with a crucified Christ. On an area of seven hectares, an urban landscape has been modeled on ancient Jerusalem – and made out of plastic.

Tierra Santa is a kind of Disneyland for faithful Christians, and unique in this respect. In the Easter week alone, this "Holy Land" receives more than 35,000 visitors, eager to experience live the crucifixion of Jesus Christ. This is not a joke! Alongside colorful plaster figures, employees of the theme park dressed in Bedouin robes re-enact stories from the Bible at various points in the park. Starting with the birth of the Messiah after they pass through the entrance, visitors are guided through the whole life of Christ from beginning to end. One of the highlights is, of course, the resurrection. Just before the clock strikes the hour, a larger-than-lifesize figure of Jesus that can wink its eyes, but does not otherwise seem especially dynamic, rises up from a fake mountain. In the background, a theatrical "Hallelujah!" can be heard.

Everything has been thought of: if you have missed the Last Supper, you can assuage the pangs of hunger with pizza on the marketplace, where the stalls sell both food and biblical souvenirs. For many Roman Catholics in Buenos Aires, a trip to Tierra Santa is an opportunity to make their children better acquainted with the Bible. For others it may seem like a bizarre experience to walk through the theme park – a leisure attraction to which monks and nuns are admitted at a reduced price. Monty Python would love it – welcome to the *Life of Brian!*

Address Av. Costanera Rafael Obligado 5790, Belgrano, CABA | **Getting there** Bus 28, 33, 37, 42, 45, 107, or 160 | **Hours** Summer Fri–Sun & holidays 4–10pm, winter Fri 9am–7pm, Sat, Sun, & holidays noon–8pm | **Tip** Just behind this theme park is a large open-air pool, a rarity in Buenos Aires, and a good place to cool down if the weather is too hot.

106_The Tiniest Block

Excellent meat from the Small Apple

One very small piece of the city lies in Villa Pueyrredón. It has been shown to be the smallest block in Buenos Aires, and consists of one single modest house. This is the result of the little street Formentista crossing three blocks of houses here, and giving rise to a small island. It is called La Manzanita, the diminutive form of *manzana*, which is the Spanish word for apple. No one knows why this word was used from the 17th century onwards as a unit of measurement for blocks of houses.

In colonial urban planning, the four sides of a block were called a *cuadra*, which was 100 varas long, corresponding to approximately 83 meters. The whole block was called a *manzana*. In cities planned by the Spanish Crown, anything that deviates from this norm is a rarity. In Buenos Aires, the circular Parque Chas quarter (see ch. 76) and this example, La Manzanita, are such exceptions.

Perhaps this spot would be completely overlooked if it was not the location of Parrilla Eriberto, a traditional, authentic meat restaurant. Before that, various stores, including a hairdresser and a greengrocer, occupied the little house. The owners are said to have lived on the first floor. Today you come here for a juicy steak, grilled sausage, and innards, in the family atmosphere of the *barrio*.

There is no seating in the restaurant itself, which has just enough space for the large barbecue grill. The tables are placed all around the building, which makes you feel as if you are dining on a small traffic island. However, Villa Pueyrredón is one of the remoter districts in the city, so not many cars pass here. In the winter there is heating for the outdoor tables.

The restaurant proprietor is proud to cook his meat at La Manzanita. And before he placed his slogan on the menu, he personally paid a visit to the land registry to get confirmation: yes, this really is the smallest *manzana*!

Address Escobar 3101, Villa Pueyrredón, CABA | **Getting there** Mitre train line from Retiro toward Suárez to Miguelette, then walk beneath the General Paz Highway; bus 21, 28, 110, or 169 | **Hours** Daily 11am–midnight | **Tip** On Av. Constituyentes on the other side of the General Paz Highway (Villa Martelli, Vicente López) a huge interactive technology and science fair, Tecnópolis, is held from July to November.

107_The Torre Espacial

An abandoned amusement park with a fantastic view

There is a mysterious atmosphere at the Parque de la Ciudad: opened in 1982 on the edge of the city as an amusement park under the name Interama, this attraction never really took off. As if time had stood still, almost all of the rides and buildings are just as they were 30 years ago, only neglected and decaying. Even during daylight hours, this huge park seems like a setting for a horror film: the skeleton of a carousel, dodgem cars overgrown by shrubs, rusting roller-coaster trains, and empty fairground stalls.

The Torre Espacial is the only surviving relic of the park. Designed to look like King Arthur's sword Excalibur rammed into the ground, the tower reaches 208 meters into the sky. Only the sword shape reveals that it was once part of a failed amusement park. Most probably every resident of the city has seen it from a distance, but very few of them have ever visited it. For many years, the tower was the tallest building in Latin America, and it is still the tallest structure in Buenos Aires. The height of the viewing platform is 176 meters, equivalent to the 75th floor of a skyscraper. From the top you have a stunning panoramic view of the Argentinian capital. On clear days you can even see as far as Uruguay, 80 kilometers away. At the same time you get insights into the city that are not apparent at ground level: you see the naked contrasts between rich and poor, with the magnificent residences of Puerto Madero on the horizon and the ramshackle, low houses in the foreground that are part of the Villa 1-11-14 slum district, also known as Bajo Flores.

Although many people think they can remember seeing one, the Torre Espacial cannot boast a revolving café. This was planned, but never went into operation. As a symbol of the forgotten southern part of the city, the tower is definitely a worthwhile destination for a trip.

Address Parque de la Ciudad, Av. Escalada 4502, Villa Soldati, CABA | **Getting there** Subte E to Plaza de los Virreyes, then Pre-Metro to Parque de la Ciudad or bus 141. The Pre-Metro passes some dubious districts; if you feel unsafe, get out at Virreyes and continue by taxi. | **Hours** Sat, Sun, & holidays 10:30am–6pm, closed if it rains | **Tip** For motorsports fans: behind the park is the Buenos Aires Autodromo (open only during events: www.autodromoba.com.ar).

108_The Tres Bocas Circuit

A marsh walk

The Tigre Delta is a green lung for *porteños*. From Retiro you take a train journey of less than an hour to the harbor, where water taxis leave for the archipelago. The lines are long here on weekends. If you don't know anybody with a weekend house in the Tigre Delta, go to one of the restaurants with a camp site or to a hotel for a day or a weekend. Once you have decided on your destination, the alternatives for exploring are limited, as you are surrounded by water and will walk no more than a few paces before you encounter a sign saying "Prohibido Pasar" ("No Trespassing") on the neighboring property.

If you would like more freedom and a bit of adventure, you can explore the delta on foot in Tres Bocas. This extensive island terrain lies between four arms of the river. The best option is to take one of the water taxis to the pier at Santa Rosa. Despite the name "circuito," this is not really a circular trail. Just set off, for example straight ahead from the pier, over the first bridge, and right toward the grill restaurant and hostels. If you get lost, simply ask the locals. The paths follow the courses of rivers, across rickety wooden bridges, past weeping willows and poplars.

It is not hard to find the way back to the pier. Tres Bocas is a sleepy little village in the middle of the delta. Nevertheless, it does not lack facilities: there are several guesthouses, a restaurant, a bakery, a chapel, a pharmacy, and a doctor's surgery.

If you would like to see Tres Bocas from the river, make a phone call to Julián and Inés, who hire out boats. Once you are back on dry land, order a fresh catfish from the grill and book a room for an overnight stay, for example one of the seven rooms at Bora-Bora, which has its own little beach. Tres Bocas may be the last place where you can enjoy the atmosphere of this watery world in peace and quiet.

Address Arroyo Abra Vieja 360, Tigre, Provincia | **Getting there** Mitre train line to Tigre, or Tren de la Costa to Delta, then at Tigre harbor a ship (*lancha*) to Tres Bocas (to Santa Rosa, approx. 40 minutes) | **Hours** Boats every 30 to 60 minutes between approx. 9am & 5pm | **Tip** The former weekend house of ex-president Sarmiento is close by. It is protected by a large glass dome, a strange sight and worth a visit! (Museo de Sarmiento, Wed–Sun 10am–6pm)

109 The Universal Church

A multinational behind a fake façade

The Iglesia Universal del Reino de Dios is a charismatic Pentecostal church from Brazil with 6 million members worldwide, 500,000 of them in Argentina. Its churches, scenes of prayer, dancing, and exorcism up to four times per day, are often housed in former theaters or cinemas – the main thing is that they have a dramatic appearance.

The main Argentinian church of the movement, the Templo de la Fé on Avenida Corrientes, was once a big flower market. When the church bought it for eight million dollars in 2003, it felt that the building was not imposing enough. This decision added an amusing curiosity to the city, as the façade was extended on one side by a mirror wall. Behind it is – nothing at all! It is like a film set that could simply be pushed over. There are no rooms behind the windows on the first floor. They are simply dummies, intended to make the temple look bulkier. It is amazing that this obvious fakery has not been concealed more skilfully. Such thoughtlessness does not suit the universal church, which is known for its carefully conceived marketing strategies.

With its own television channels, publishers producing glossy literature, and travel company, the Iglesia Universal ingeniously propagates its simple message: if you donate money to the church, you will be rewarded with wealth as an expression of God's love. If you are not wealthy, then your faith must be weak, or you are possessed by devils. This promise of wealth has primarily served to make the church itself rich. In Brazil alone it has a revenue of $1.4 billion per year. Critics see it as a multinational corporation disguised as a religious community. Investigations have been under way for years against its leaders for links with drug traffickers, tax evasion, and money laundering. Goings-on like this seem to bother the faithful flock no more than the fake façade of the temple.

Address Corrientes 4070, Almagro, CABA, www.universal.org.ar | Getting there Subte B to Medrano; bus 19, 24, 71, 92, 99, 109, 124, 127, 141, or 168 | Hours Building: open for visitors 8am–8pm, mass is held several times daily | Tip Around the corner is the alternate tango club La Catedral (Sarmiento 4006, daily 8pm–4am).

110_Velatropa

A green social experiment on the campus

Surrounded by highways and the concrete blocks of the university campus, the green village of Velatropa lies hidden behind bushes and trees. Unnoticed by millions of city inhabitants, a small group of young people are trying to lead a self-sufficient, sustainable, and ecological life as far as possible. The site was originally intended for a new faculty building, for which the concrete foundations have already been poured. But nothing happened here for decades, and heaps of rubbish piled up. When a group of students occupied the land in 2007, they cleaned it up, planted trees, and built small dwellings, as well as a biological toilet.

Velatropa became a kind of nature reserve with a built-in social experiment. The people who run it aim to set a good example, living in harmony with nature, even in the city. One of them took this so seriously that he hung a small house from the tops of the trees, and has to climb a rope to reach it. Most of the *velatroperos*, however, alternate between "normal" urban life and this social project. To become part of the community, you have to come with an idea that you want to contribute. This was the origin of the wood-burning baking oven, a vegetable garden, a common room with library, a bike workshop, and a solar cooker.

Visitors are welcome at any time – in theory, at least. Every one of the residents has his or her own opinion about what Velatropa is and should be. This means that the experiment is dynamic, on the one hand, but several principles such as regular committee meetings and strict adherence to the Mayan calendar have been abandoned. Whenever you come here, you will meet someone who is willing to show you around. The ecological village can be found by taking a small beaten path behind the northernmost building of the Ciudad Universitaria, simply following the line of painted plant pots.

Address Ciudad Universitaria, Nuñez, CABA | **Getting there** Belgrano Norte train line from Retiro to Ciudad Universitaria; bus 28, 33, 37, 42, 45, 107, or 160 | **Hours** Accessible in daytime; for photography, ask for permission | **Tip** On the other side of the highway stands the country's most famous and biggest football stadium: El Monumental, the home of River Plate, with its museum (Av. Figueroa Alcorta 7597, daily 10am–6pm, hourly tours of the stadium).

111 Villa 31

A look behind the façade

Is this not the well-known tourist attraction El Caminito with its brightly colored houses in the La Boca harbor quarter? The façade looks deceptively similar, but behind it lies Villa 31, one of the largest areas of unofficial housing in Buenos Aires. In 2009, the Kirchner government decided to improve the quality of life here. One of its measures was to paint the façade. Another was to build playgrounds. Some welcomed these improvements, while others complained that they amounted merely to cosmetic treatment for poverty. The real problems here are much more basic: unemployment, lack of drinking water, and poor health care.

More than 40,000 people live in this *villa miseria*, as the slum districts are called that are elsewhere known as favelas or shanty towns. Every day, thousands drive past them on the Illia highway, and the exit of the terminal for overland buses is situated right next to the colorful façades. The brick-built houses with tin roofs rise up to five stories high, crammed in between the tracks of the Retiro train stations and the port. The narrow clay roads are three kilometers long. In the background rise the luxury hotels and apartments of Recoleta. Villa 31 is the symbol of social inequality and injustice in Argentina.

A square meter of building land would cost several thousand dollars here. This is not the least important reason why Villa 31 has been a thorn in the flesh of many generations of politicians since it came into existence. The residents have been forcibly evicted several times, for example for the football World Cup in 1978.

Several of the villas are in the hands of the drug-dealing mafia. Gang warfare with fatalities breaks out here with great regularity. However, most of the inhabitants of Villa 31 are people who work for a living in the service economy: cleaners, drivers, and domestic servants.

Address Calle 4 and Carlos H. Perette, Retiro, CABA | **Getting there** In addition to long-distance buses that drive to the terminal, buses 33 and 45 pass Villa 31 | **Note** You often pass Villa 31 by bus or taxi. We have included it in order to report about the social situation in the villas. For security reasons and out of respect for the residents, we do not advise making a visit. | **Tip** Several NGOs work in the city's *villas miserias*. The aim of the project www.caminosdelavilla.org is to make these settlements visible on maps, from which they are often left out. It is worth taking a look at this website!

1
58
108
TIGRE
Río Luján
SAN FERNANDO
84
19
5
37
SAN ISIDRO
9
MARTÍNEZ
BOULOGNE
9
VICENTE LÓPEZ
3
VILLA BALLESTER
83
VILLA BOSCH
COLEGIALES
92
CASEROS
EL PALOMAR
68
CABALLITO
7
1
61
34
MATADEROS
41
LOMAS
DEL MIRADOR
107
N
0
0,93 mi
SAN JUSTO
17

2
4
5
BUENOS AIRES
MONSERRAT
1
VALENTÍN ALSINA
97
97
VILLA DOMINICO
1
79
N
0
0,93 mi

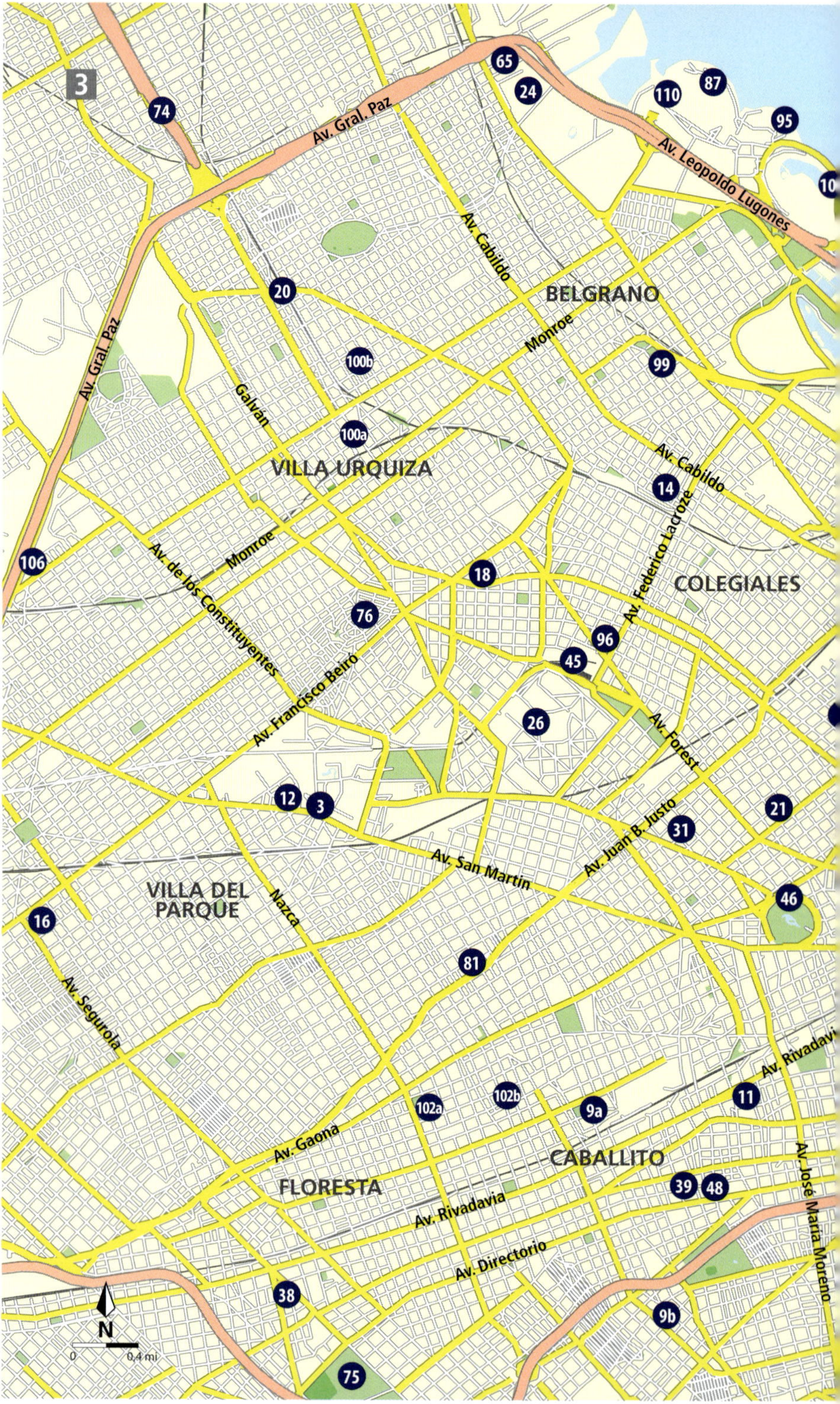

3
Av. Gral. Paz
Av. Cabildo
Av. Leopoldo Lugones
BELGRANO
Monroe
Galván
VILLA URQUIZA
Av. Cabildo
Av. Federico Lacroze
COLEGIALES
Av. de los Constituyentes
Av. Francisco Beiró
Av. Forest
Av. Juan B. Justo
Av. San Martín
VILLA DEL PARQUE
Nazca
Av. Segurola
Av. Rivadavia
Av. Gaona
CABALLITO
FLORESTA
Av. Rivadavia
Av. Directorio
Av. José María Moreno
N
0
0,4 mi
65
24
110
87
95
74
20
100b
100a
99
14
106
18
76
96
45
26
12
3
31
21
46
16
81
102a
102b
9a
11
39
48
38
9b
75

4
5
Autopista Arturo Illia
Av. del Libertador
Av. Santa Fe
Av. Santa Fe
Av. Córdoba
Av. Medrano
Av. Pueyrredon
Av. Callao
BUENOS AIRES
Av. Corrientes
BALVANERA
Av. Rivadavia
ALMAGRO
MONSERRAT
Av. Entre Ríos
Av. Independencia
Av. San Juan
Autopista 25 de Mayo
Av. Juan de Garay
Defensa
Av. Boedo
Av. Jujuy
Brown
Av. Almirante
29
85
47
43
71
59
111
35
69
50
98
56
109
62
33
28
90
91
25
103
104
22
82
77
7
N
0
0,4 mi

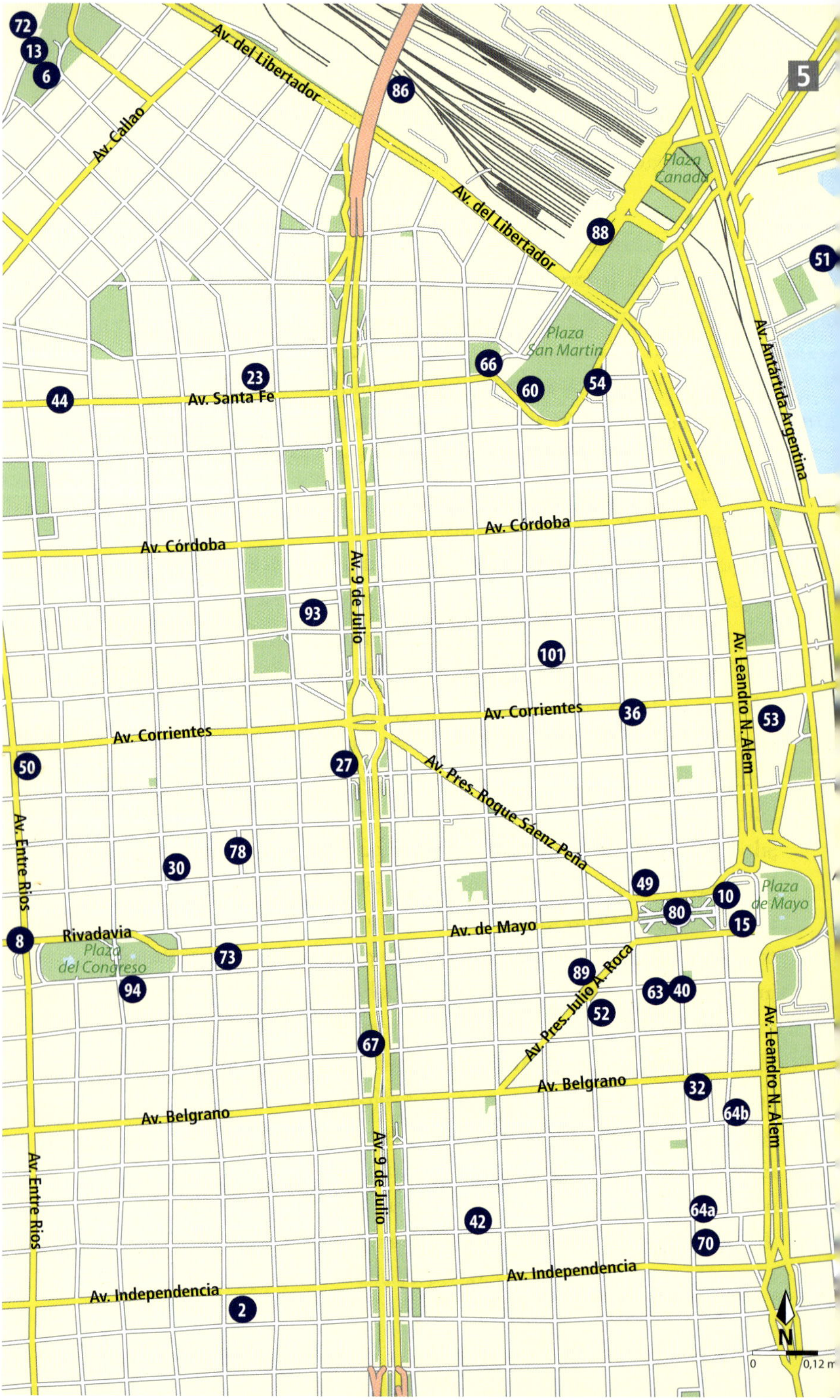

5
Av. del Libertador
Av. Callao
Plaza Canadá
Plaza San Martín
Av. Santa Fe
Av. Antártida Argentina
Av. Córdoba
Av. 9 de Julio
Av. Leandro N. Alem
Av. Corrientes
Av. Pres. Roque Sáenz Peña
Av. Entre Ríos
Plaza de Mayo
Rivadavia
Av. de Mayo
Plaza del Congreso
Av. Pres. Julio A. Roca
Av. Belgrano
Av. Independencia
N
0
0,12 m
72
13
6
86
88
51
66
23
44
60
54
93
101
36
53
50
27
78
30
49
10
80
15
8
73
94
89
63
40
52
67
32
64b
64a
42
70
2

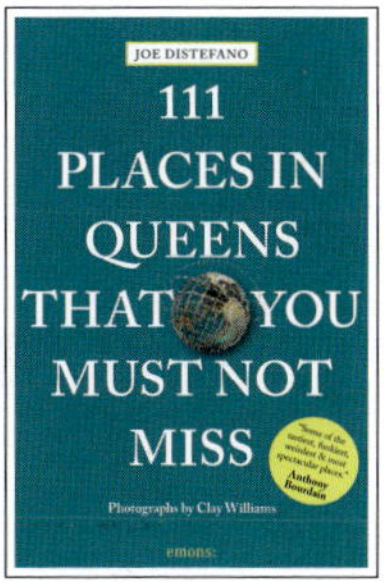

Joe DiStefano
111 PLACES IN QUEENS THAT YOU MUST NOT MISS
ISBN 978-3-7408-0020-8

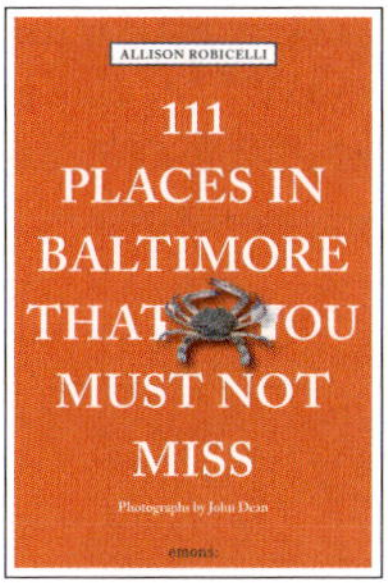

Allison Robicelli
111 PLACES IN BALTIMORE THAT YOU MUST NOT MISS
ISBN 978-3-7408-0158-8

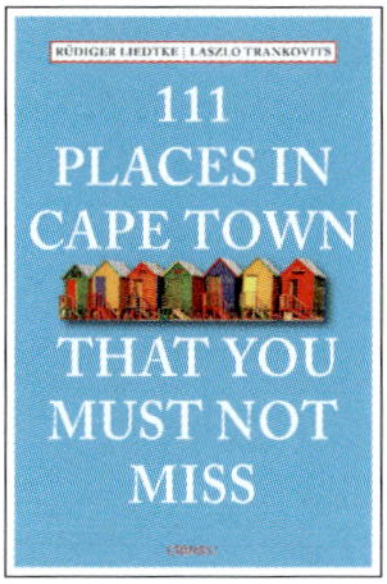

Rüdiger Liedtke,
Laszlo Trankovits
111 PLACES IN CAPE TOWN THAT YOU MUST NOT MISS
ISBN 978-3-95451-610-0

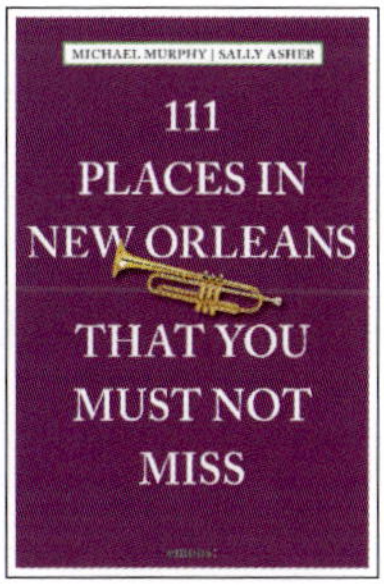

Sally Asher, Michael Murphy
111 PLACES IN NEW ORLEANS THAT YOU MUST NOT MISS
ISBN 978-3-95451-645-2

Laurel Moglen, Julia Posey
111 PLACES IN LOS ANGELES THAT YOU SHOULDN'T MISS
ISBN 978-3-95451-884-5

Beate C. Kirchner
111 PLACES IN RIO DE JANEIRO THAT YOU MUST NOT MISS
ISBN 978-3-7408-0262-2

John Sykes
111 PLACES IN LONDON THAT YOU SHOULDN'T MISS
ISBN 978-3-95451-346-8

Gordon Streisand
111 PLACES IN MIAMI AND THE KEYS THAT YOU MUST NOT MISS
ISBN 978-3-95451-644-5

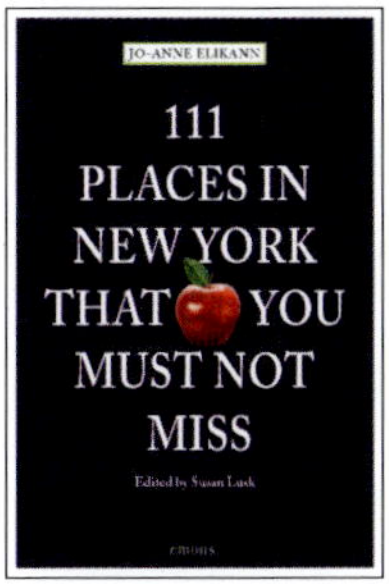

Jo-Anne Elikann
111 PLACES IN NEW YORK THAT YOU MUST NOT MISS
ISBN 978-3-95451-052-8

Dirk Engelhardt
111 PLACES IN BARCELONA THAT YOU MUST NOT MISS
ISBN 978-3-95451-353-6

Rüdiger Liedtke
111 PLACES ON MALLORCA THAT YOU SHOULDN'T MISS
ISBN 978-3-95451-281-2

Marcus X. Schmid
111 PLACES IN ISTANBUL THAT YOU MUST NOT MISS
ISBN 978-3-95451-423-6

Sybil Canac, Renée Grimaud, Katia Thomas
111 PLACES IN PARIS THAT YOU SHOULDN'T MISS
ISBN 978-3-7408-0159-5

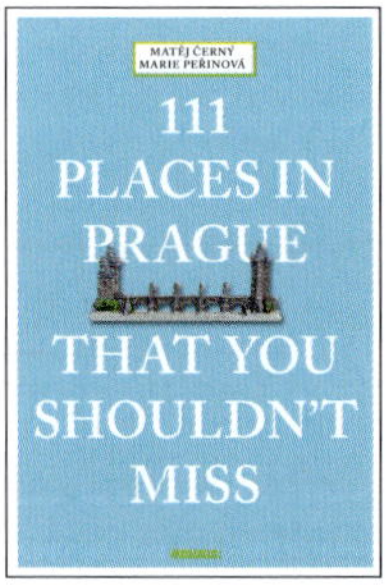

Matěj Černý, Marie Peřinová
111 PLACES IN PRAGUE THAT YOU SHOULDN'T MISS
ISBN 978-3-7408-0144-1

Sharon Fernandes
111 PLACES IN NEW DELHI THAT YOU MUST NOT MISS
ISBN 978-3-95451-648-3

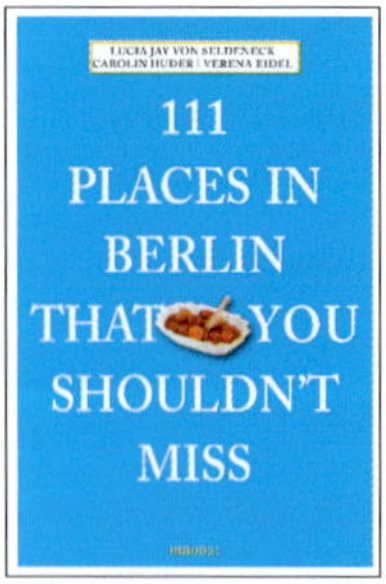

Lucia Jay von Seldeneck, Carolin Huder, Verena Eidel
111 PLACES IN BERLIN THAT YOU SHOULDN'T MISS
ISBN 978-3-95451-208-9

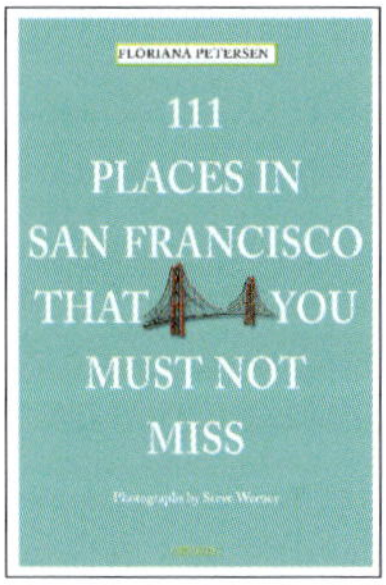

Floriana Petersen
111 PLACES IN SAN FRANCISCO THAT YOU MUST NOT MISS
ISBN 978-3-95451-609-4

Kathrin Bielfeldt, Raymond Wong
111 PLACES IN HONG KONG THAT YOU SHOULDN'T MISS
ISBN 978-3-95451-936-1

Notes

Terms:

Buenos Aires consists of the urban area called Ciudad Autónoma de Buenos Aires (CABA) or Capital, and the metropolitan area, called Gran Buenos Aires or Provincia.

Distances are given in *cuadras*. A *cuadra* is one side of a block of buildings, and measures approximately 100 meters. A complete block is called a *manzana* (see ch. 106 in this book).

Transport:

The subway system, the Subte, links up the most important districts in the Capital. The bus system is good in both the Capital and the Provincia. The bus stops have no names, but are called by the street junctions. Buses listed in this book usually go to within 300 meters of the place that is described. At kiosks in the city center you can get the Guía-T city map, which gives all Subte lines and bus routes.

Suburban trains connect the Provincia with the four main stations in the Capital. For some of the more remote places in this book, the suburban lines are the quickest means of transport. Travel planning on the internet: www.comollego.ba.gob.ar (only for the Capital, also available as an app), www.omnilineas.com.ar/buenos-aires/colectivos (available in English for the Capital and Provincia).

Safety:

In Buenos Aires, as in any other large city in the world, there are safe and unsafe areas. The relatively high level of social inequality and poverty leads to a high crime rate in some districts. The degree of risk depends on several factors, including visitors' knowledge of the city. We regard visits to the places in this book as safe, and draw attention to special situations. In general, be alert, pay heed to common sense, and note any travel warnings of your country's diplomatic service.

Acknowledgements

We would like to thank Simon Simko (Instagram @drones.arg) for the aerial shot in chapter 97.

The authors

Benjamin Haas, born in Tuttlingen an der Donau in Germany, is a cultural anthropologist and student of Latin America. He did voluntary service in Buenos Aires in 2005, and was a journalist there for a German-language newspaper, the *Argentinisches Tageblatt*. Later he worked for several years as a freelance journalist, for the Deutsche Presse-Agentur among other agencies. Today he is employed as a researcher at the University of Cologne and does freelance work in political education.

Leonie Friedrich, born in Hamburg, Germany, lived for a year in Buenos Aires to carry out voluntary service. Since 2013 she has worked as a freelance midwife in Bonn.

Since their first stay in the city on the Río de la Plata, where they met in 2008, both authors have returned there frequently. They are pleased to receive comments about this book.
(111PlacesBsAs@gmail.com)